CHAPTER 1

INTRODUCTION

Problem

Why should we try to predict the future and what do we gain by trying? The United States Army constantly searches for ways to improve its military organizations and operational efficiency. But, this is a difficult process and it takes years to implement. As we move into the twenty-first century, the Army must examine its structure and doctrine to remain relevant. As part of this effort, the thesis question asks: Will the Infantry squad of the Army of excellence fit into the Army force of 2015?

The Army After Next doctrinal interpretation of future combat is captured below in a newspaper article that may be written in the year 2016. This vignette may answer why it is important to continue to develop forces for the future.

Vignette: Army After Next 2016

Dateline, 10 November 2016. "Battle Force Tested." (Kosovo). AP. At the behest of the United Nations Security Counsel the United States has become embroiled in a combat operation now being called Operation Vigilant Shield. On 1 November, Army Lieutenant General Franklin Lewis, Commander 22d Joint Battle Force (JBF), the Army's premier rapid deployment contingency force, received notification from the National Command Authority to prepare for possible missions in the wartorn nation of Kosovo. The National Command Authority (NCA) identified the operation's strategic goals as one, to prevent Kosovo leaders who possess regional hegemonic goals from conducting raids on neighboring countries nuclear production facilities, and two, to prevent nuclear terror attacks on the United States and NATO allies. Further, success in the Vigilant Shield operation would diminish the chances that the KLF could secure regional primacy over the national resources in the area.

The KLF (Kosovo Liberation Front) has recently modernized several components of their military war machine. They have acquired long range precision missiles and information gathering assets through France and other international dealers. Their most current acquisition was a space intelligence/monitor that provides the KLF early warning of any airborne or

1

seaborne intruder to their international borders. It also integrates several systems to engage forces as they arrive in country with immediate air defense artillery (ADA) precision-guided rockets, mobile armored land forces, and various forms of attack aircraft.

In an attempt to preempt the KLF's effort, which is backed by the powerful nation of Iraq, the 22d JBF deployed on a forced entry operation, described as Strategic Preclusion by the NCA. Strategic Preclusion is characterized by a preemptive strike first use of force, aimed at limited physical destruction and maximum military paralysis in the accomplishment of an assigned mission.

The purpose of the operation Vigilant Shield was to introduce forces into the area, as a prelude to a UN occupation force, and conduct operational maneuver to destroy the long-range nuclear missile threat of the KLF, as well as to destroy the KLF's command, control, communication, computer and intelligence systems. The operation's ultimate objective was to bring the KLF to the political bargaining table.

The 22d JBF's mission entailed rapid maneuver to seize and destroy multiple key targets in rapid succession. The operation conducted by this force took place over an area that covered 1200 square miles. Some targets were over 100 miles away from the initial point of entry. The simultaneity of the attacks crippled the KLF and forced them to petition for peace after only 4 days of fighting.[1]

Losses to American soldiers totaled 14, most of which occurred when an Eagle VTLC (Vertical takeoff and Landing Craft) was shot down after inserting ground troops on a critical objective site. For an operation of this magnitude losses were also uncharacteristically low for the KLF. Army spokesperson MAJ Shelia Carmicheal stated, "The goal of this operation was not to destroy the KLF forces, but to annihilate his ability to resist US forces facing him in his country. Within days the KLF faced continuing the fight without any of its major defense systems intact or bargaining for peace with the United States. The KLF knew that we were dedicated to accomplishing our mission by all means available."

Lieutenant General Lewis, commander of the 'Battle Force' said, "The key to this operation was to enter the country quickly with enough force to protect us for as long as it took to destroy his nerve center and make him hurt."

The 22d JBF conducted a strategic infiltration with a battalion of armored vehicles and two battalions of Mobile Infantry (MI).[2] The first MI battalion conducted a parachute assault to seize an airfield strategically located in the center of the country. Next a battalion of armored vehicles sustained the airhead with the new M-21 family of vehicles, while the second battalion of MI set out on 12 separate missions to destroy power facilities, communications nodes, headquarters, satellite communications centers, weapons of mass destruction sites, and strategic missile sights.

LTG Lewis said, "We needed the M-21 to hold the airfield as well as to destroy targets with our missiles as soon as we arrived in country. The M-21s were a great force multiplier and made this operation feasible. With the tanks, we had an armored force on the ground that could defeat their precision guided munitions (PGMs) and destroy their older armored vehicles from a distance. Fortunately we could fit a platoon of the new M-21s into each our C-17s, which landed after the first Mobile Infantry Battalion conducted the airborne assault."[3]

LTG Lewis continued, "The key to the operation was to deploy the remainder of the Mobile Infantry Battalions strategically, directly onto targets in country. The Eagles (The Army's newest strategic/tactical transport vertical takeoff and landing craft) were used to transport squads and platoons of the 4-21 MI, undetected to their targets at the same time we were securing the airfield. After 3-17 MI conducted their initial airborne assault, augmented by the WAM (Wide Angle Munition)[4], they trans-loaded into Falcons (The forces new Joint Transport Rotor) to fly to their subsequent objectives. They executed their missions from the airfield during the remainder of the operation.[5] Our force was exhausted at the end of the operation because of the tempo and intensity of the battles, I know the KLF had to have been overwhelmed by the intensity of the fight."

"The key to this operation was that we overcame the enemy's strengths by relying on old fashion vertical envelopment with light forces which allowed us to move undetected to the enemy's pressure points. We then used our light forces to designate precise targets in built up areas for the M-21's. Both MI battalions were successful when they engaged forces in heavy close fighting on their objectives," said the Joint Strike Force's CSM Greenway.

SSG Zim, a squad leader in Company C, 4-21 MI, tells his story. We were on the Eagles for close to ten hours before we finally got to our objective, which was a satellite communications site. Our landing site kept changing during the flight because of the KLF air defense, but I was able to keep up with things over the net on the screen (Commander's station of the Land Warrior Computer). I knew I would touch down on a landing zone, walk about 2 clicks to our target, and then designate targets for the MLRS rockets from the airfield out of the fired from the M-21s.

All went well until we ran into a couple of KLF at an outpost as we were maneuvering to clear the target that had been destroyed by our rockets. One of my teams was ready to clear rooms looking for survivors to bring back as prisoners for interrogation. We switched our OICWs (Objective Integrated Combat Weapons) to 5.56 heavy as we always do to clear rooms. Then we maneuvered the way the drill called for but two my boys in A team got popped. The team still had the men to drive on with their mission as the lead team and my LW hooah (Land Warrior equipped soldier) from B-team slapped a 911[6] wrap on both of them and we carted them out with the two PWs on the Eagles when we exfilled. It was pretty hairy but my PL was only a couple of clicks away on another platoon Objective that called for two squads. I knew if I needed help that he could send an Eagle right to me or pop over with a squad to save us from real trouble. Ends up my platoon leader had me on his screen the whole time and knew our situation when it went bad. As a matter of fact the platoon sent the Eagle to the PZ to pick me up before I called for it. Both of my hooah's made it.

This was another successful mission for the Joint Strike Force and the first time they deployed with the M-21s. General Peter Lyncher, Chairman of the Joint Chiefs of Staff said, "The Joint Strike Force has validated our ability to go in big, strike hard and accomplish the mission with little cost of American lives. He continued, We hope in the future that we can perfect our stealth technology to keep our birds from getting shot down in high risk areas. The lose of one American soldier is too many.

So now the issue of how to deal with the KLF is back into the policy makers hands. A US stability force as part of the UN peace enforcement team will replace the JBF. The JBF will return home to prepare for the next time they are called to protect the world from the forces of evil.

Combat in the early part of the twenty-first century could feasibly take the form illustrated by this futuristic vignette. How do we develop the forces to execute this form of revolutionary warfare? The force development to accomplish the strategic preclusion[7] described above has significant challenges. It is indeed difficult to change without a global conflict to challenge us and to test and shape theory, doctrine and organizational structure. For as Liddell Hart so aptly phrased, "before a war military science seems like a real science, like astronomy, but after a war it seems more like astrology."[8] Before World War I, the world's major military powers studied major battles to determine how best to prepare their forces to fight in the future. Their classrooms were the battlefields of the Russo-Japanese War and the Franco Prussian War. According to John English, as of 1888 the "Masses of manpower had, in fact, surrendered its position of superiority on the field of battle to concentrated firepower."[9] Wars in the late 1880s were indeed comparable to the conflict they foreshadowed in World War I.

Between the First World War I and World War II, the great nations wrestled with integrating advances in mechanical automation into the military applications. The nations, that would eventually become the Allies in World War II, invested considerable effort experimenting with the use of the tank and other modern technologies in war

4

fighting applications. But, their failure to recognize the utility of their findings and effect organization structural and doctrinal reforms caused them to lag behind the Germans at the outset of the war in military supremacy. Conversely, the Germans took many Allied experimental findings and incorporated them into their military doctrine, by way of visionaries, such as General Heinz Guderian. The impact of the Allied failure to evolve was obvious, at the outset of the Second World War in 1939.[10]

In fact, the United States was as guilty of military stagnation as any country as James Fitzsimonds and Jan Van Tol describe in their article "Revolution in Military Affairs," Joint Force Quarterly. They illustrate their point with the following passage about one of our greatest war fighters.

> Stationed at Camp Meade, Maryland just after World War I, Dwight Eisenhower and George Patton both began articles for military journals describing their experiments utilizing new doctrine for the employment of tanks. "Then I was called before the Chief of Infantry," Eisenhower later recalled. " I was told that my ideas were not only wrong, but dangerous and that henceforth I would keep them to myself. Particularly, I was not to publish anything incompatible with solid infantry doctrine. If I did, I would be hauled before a courts-marshal.[11]

If military theorists cling to traditional parochial thought and stifle initiative in their community, it is especially difficult to facilitate effective advancements in warfighting. It is hard to convince an organization that it needs to improve when it has displayed excellence, similar to the American armed forces after the Gulf War. But, the geostrategic environment is constantly changing and technological advances continue. Liddell Hart observed this attitude and wrote, "It is not difficult to put new ideas into the military mind, but it is difficult to get the old ones out."[12]

The problem of preparing a military force for future conflicts may best be compared to a sports analogy. It is extremely difficult to prepare a team for a game in which you do not know whom your future opponent will be or, for that matter, which sport you will play. Military theorists are troubled with having to forecast the forces they will have to fight in the future to shape their force today. Raymond Finch illustrates the problem in the passage below. He describes the challenges contemporary doctrine writers have forecasting threat based on trends in the geostrategic environment. He believes that theorists fixate on building an adversarial threat army in our own image regardless of the indicators.

> At this belief's core is the tenant that militaries fight other militaries—soldiers fight other soldiers [or that] uniformed players only compete against an opposing team. Until the beginning of the 20th century, the game of war was pretty well confined to the battlefield. Even with the advent of modern weaponry, the belief has persisted that to win the game, one team must defeat the other. To win a war means defeating the opponent's military.
> As we move into the 21st century, the game's structure is changing. With a weakening of the national state, Carl Von Clausewitz's dictum that war is an extension of [state] politics may no longer be valid. As the state has deteriorated, the opposing team's military has broken up, and some of the players have moved up into the stands to wreak havoc there.[13]

The issue is to integrate contemporary and future advances in technology into the armed forces and hopefully bring about a revolution in military affairs (RMA). The Russians coined the term Revolution in Military Affairs to describe the changes created by the advent of nuclear weapons and ballistic missiles into the strategic defense picture. The term revolution was used because the collective body of Russian military strategists believed that nuclear arms and missiles would so drastically change the conduct of war in the future that they would have to alter their doctrine to address the tactical, operational, and strategic levels of war.[14] Training and Doctrine Command (TRADOC) Pamphlet 525-5, our U.S. Army's doctrinal vision manual that provides guidance to the force for future doctrine development.[15] "Innovations in technology and doctrine are the

6

harbingers of change in warfare. Dramatic developments in both of these areas have resulted in a revolution in military affairs."[16] TRADOC Pam 525-5 refers to the RMA as a Military Technical Revolution (MTR) and it defines it as a holistic occurrence involving much more than technological change. It states that an MTR "occurs when the application of new technologies into military systems combines with innovative operational concepts or organizational adaptation to alter fundamentally the character and conduct of military operations.... What is revolutionary about an MTR is not the speed with which the change takes place, but rather the magnitude of the change itself. Mere technological improvements do not constitute an MTR."[17] Simply, an RMA or MTR is a fundamental comprehensive change in the way war is conducted that makes the wars of the past obsolete. Successful RMAs, such as the Germans accomplished with blitzkrieg in World War II and the United States attained by employing the atomic bomb, show that the force that adapts technology quicker and more thoroughly into their doctrine will have a distinct advantage over their opponents.

The United States armed forces are on the verge of the next RMA. This RMA, which integrates information dominance, space supremacy, lightweight digital technology, and alternate energy sources, is potentially greater than any before. So it is necessary to challenge traditional thought at every level of the organization. To ensure success with the revolution, we must examine all organizations starting at the ground level and working up. Thus, the thesis research question: Will the current Infantry squad organization and composition fit into the United States Army force of 2015?

Background

The inspiration for this study stems from the discovery of the Army's new technological developments for the infantryman. The Infantry Center briefed the Command and General Staff College infantry students on the land warrior (LW) system and associated innovations at the beginning of the academic year. Chapter 4 will discuss the components of the LW System, which shocked the author's Infantry peers. The LW System at first appears cumbersome, fragile, and too heavy for a soldier to carry into combat. The thirty infantry majors in the audience were mortified that the Army would support a system that is obviously not built for the average infantryman. Overheard were comments to the effect, "This thing will never work.... Its too heavy for the soldier to carry into combat.... The thing will break as soon as a soldier gets the thing in the field." And if we plan to fight the next war the way that we fought the Vietnam War, I believe their observations may be accurate. So I began to question my peers thought process and decided maybe this equipment may help us change the way we fight.

The next significant piece of background information comes from my own field observations. During my last assignment, it was my privilege to work in a unit that truly could operate effectively at night. This fact was not necessarily because of an extraordinary tactical acumen, rather it was primarily because of the equipment we acquired while I was there. As a second lieutenant entering the 7th Infantry Division in 1988, we boasted as our motto, "We own the night." It was curious that we claimed to own the night, when only a fraction of our soldiers within our tactical units were allocated night vision goggles or scopes. We trained at night and could navigate and move fairly well, but the naked eye and metal rifle sights dictated the limitations of the

8

rifleman's night marksmanship. The soldiers had to be within twenty-five to fifty meters from the target to effectively engage and destroy it. The Army of Excellence of the eighties espoused that it would dominate potential enemies in all night operations because of our technological advantage in night vision. This may have been the case for mounted and aerial systems but it was surely not the case for light infantry units, particularly with the increase in night vision proliferation throughout the world.

As a Company Commander in the 3d Ranger Battalion in 1998 I witnessed the acquisition of night vision equipment that allowed us to outfit every Ranger with night vision devices, most of which we could mount on their helmets. Also, laser-aiming devices augmented the majority of weapons systems within the battalion. This combination allowed the squads and platoons to effectively engage targets, on the move at night, from distances in excess of 150 meters. Additionally, the situational awareness of the force increased which made it possible for the squads to effectively fire and maneuver at night for the first time. For example, the squad automatic riflemen were unencumbered by the traditional scope mounted on their M-249 squad automatic weapon (SAW). In the past while moving with his fire team the SAW gunner could not see because he was not allocated helmet mounted PVS-7s. The old PVS-4 night scope that he was issued required the gunner to engage targets in the prone while looking through the scope then pick up and move on the order of his team leader and move forward with the team, now effectively blind. By mounting a laser on the weapon and providing the SAW gunner with helmet-mounted PVS-7s he was able to observe the actions of his fire team while providing them with effective suppressive from a variety of firing positions.

Second, is the influence of the fictional novel <u>Starship Troopers</u>, by Robert Heinlein. Heinlein's book, written in 1959, forecasted the nature of futuristic warfare as planet earth and her people struggled in a war for survival against alien creatures. He brilliantly portrays the infantryman of the future and stresses the importance of realistic nuts and bolts basic training. Heinlein's mobile infantrymen (MI) deployed into combat from space ships via airborne pods and equipped with power suits that carried advanced communications and weapons packages. The basic unit in the MI was the squad and the training for a position in the unit was extremely physically challenging and competitive. Despite all the high tech gadgetry carried by the MI, Heinlein advocated extreme mental and physical military training to prepare soldiers for the inevitable stress that they would experience in combat.

Heinlein's insights inspired me to ponder the organizational and doctrinal possibilities for our future force. I began to question the attitudes contemporary Infantry leaders displayed about the Land Warrior System. Indeed as many of my peers believe, the system may be off the mark if applied using present doctrine, but again I asked, could it work for a warrior now or in the year 2015 if we used different tactics?

<u>Limitations</u>

The ability to test squad performance in tactical or live simulations poses a limitation to this study. This constraint is imposed by the physical separation of the author from the development center at the Infantry School and by the lack of tangible data from TRADOC System Manager (TSM) directed field tests. The 3d Battalion, 325th Parachute Infantry Regiment (PIR), has conducted field tests at Fort Bragg using

10

LW equipment, but these tests have been focused on the development of individual components of the system. The system's technical civilian developers at Ratheon, in an attempt to work the bugs out of each component, have informally gathered the findings of these tests to assist in their product's development and not published many results for evaluation.[18]

Other limitations were a lack of pure empirical performance data of the components of the Land Warrior System and a lack of physical organizational testing at the platoon or squad level. The Simulations Center at Fort Benning has conducted tests of the Land Warrior System, using virtual simulation (mathematical modeling), but the results are difficult to correlate directly to the infantry squad.[19] Without the written test results and AAR comments from the Infantry Center, much of my findings have been subject to conjecture and second-hand source information gained from interviews.

Delimitations

This paper explores an infantry squad organization the Army could apply to each of the five present forms of Infantry units; Ranger, Air Assault, Airborne, Light, and Mechanized. Many argue for specification within future Infantry units with independent organizations and doctrine, but time and space limit their research here. Thus, I will use the "One Infantry" philosophy espoused by the current Chief of the Infantry, Major General Ernst.[20]

Further, I have imposed several limitations on this study to adequately reduce the scope of the paper. These include: the study of the infantry's future forms of conveyance, the exploration or consideration of technology applications beyond those of the Land Warrior System and related programs, the training requirements of the future squad, a detailed examination of the tactics of squad employment or future battle drills, the recruitment policy to provide extremely qualified men to operate sophisticated systems, Army manning policies, logistics alternatives, squad integration into the platoon or company, and exploration of special forces units.

Many of the identified delimitations may serve as the basis for future research questions and other study, which I will further outline in the conclusion chapter.

Significance

The phenomenon of a Revolution in Military Affairs is a driving force that underscores the significance of this thesis. The study of the definition and the implications of an RMA is important to the essence of the Army's being. Since there is often extended time between major wars to test the validity of developing operational systems and doctrine it is foolish to stick to the old ways purely based on ignorance and the inability or inflexibility to explore new ideas. Stagnation, especially in the light of new leap ahead technology, can be catastrophic.[21] As illustrated by the futuristic vignette, the potential for a RMA that may occur via new technology should cause sound military organizations to consider doctrinal and organizational changes. As witnessed throughout history, countries that fail to develop their forces in peace are susceptible to domination by peer competitors in war. The fact that the United States is presently without a peer competitor makes the need for exploration and experimentation of new systems and organizations seem obscure, futile, and wasteful to the casual observer. Once a major force emerges on the global scene, as Germany did in 1939, it may be too

12

late to react and develop the systems required to win the next war.[22] Also, development of future military theory from the field is valuable to the agencies charged with developing systems. Project managers rarely employ theorists in their offices and are understaffed to complete the task themselves.[23] Thus, the study of theoretical military doctrine and organization is a relevant topic for thesis discovery.

---

[1]United States Army Training and Doctrine Command, Annual Report on the Army After Next (Fort Monroe, VA: 7 December 1998). [Online] Available: www.tradoc.army.mil/dcsdoc/aan.htm, 10 Jan 98. p. 11. Army After Next doctrine advocates the development of Battle Force organizations as the most modernized element within the future hybrid forces of the United States Army. They will be designed with revolutionary capabilities and concepts enabled by cutting edge technologies. Battle Forces will execute strategic preclusion and strategic maneuver for the National Command Authority, augmented by detailed intelligence and planning by the highest levels in the JCS. These forces will leverage superior intelligence gathering and management capabilities to conduct strategic movement directly onto tactical targets. The Battle Force will stream line the entire system of deployment, to include logistic support to facilitate forward presence and mission accomplishment in days or weeks rather than months. Following early entry this force would conduct vertical or near vertical maneuver to operational depths and pose great threats to enemy maneuver formations and critical nodes.

[2]LTC John Medve USA, The Annual Report on The Army After Next Project to the Chief of Staff of the Army. (Fort Monroe, VA: 1 August 1997), 15. Data from the AAN winter war games showed that rapid strategic maneuver was paramount to gaining superiority and presence in enemy terrain. This calls for establishing a force on the ground capable of securing itself and executing combat missions within two weeks of notification, rather than the months it presently takes. The obvious conclusion from this, is that a force must be introduced that is capable of rapid strategic maneuver and has the protection and firepower to make a difference in country and a small tailored logistics package to support it.

[3]Shirley Eugene Terrence. "21st Century Mobile weapon Platform." Research Development, Acquisition: Army RD&A. January-February 1999, 27-28. The Army is developing a vehicle called model 21-C. It will have a low silhouette and no gun tube or turret. It will be able to alter its thermal signature by cloaking itself in an electronically controlled umbrella. To counter thermal-guided munitions it will have passive decoys to confuse the munitions. It can project a thermal-cloud around itself to create a decoy that can appear to sensors as hot or cold dependant on the threat. It can physically alter its shape. It maintains armor, only around the two-man crew, made up of metal and honey combed polymers that efficiently dissipate energy. It weighs one-third as much as the old

M1 tank. It rides on eight road wheels that can adjust to different types of terrain. The production of this Tank is doable now with today's technology. It can deploy with a light force. The two-man crew can shoot for remote sensors with antiaircraft, artillery (MLRS) or anti-armor systems from the removable internal launch tubes.

[4]WAM is a dismounted man portable tank killing system in development. It can be placed on the ground in front of friendly troops and senses the approach of an armored vehicle. Based on the range data loaded by the unit, it will engage vehicles with a heat-seeking missile from the top down. This system gives the light forced entry units a tank killing capability.

[5]United States Army Training and Doctrine Command. Annual Report on the Army After Next (Fort Monroe, VA., 7 December 1998). [Online] Available: www.tradoc.army.mil/dcsdoc/aan.htm, 10 Jan 98. p 10. The VTOL (Vertical Takeoff and landing craft) and the JTR (Joint Transport Rotor) will enable units to cross the killing zone at speeds over 3 times as fast as today's transports, possibly using stealth technologies to infiltrate small unit forces to the decisive point on the battlefield.

[6] The 991 bandage is the future Medical sustainment kit. The 911 is a bandage that comes loaded with pain killers, blood coagulants, antibiotic, and seals itself to the good flesh around the wound. Initial estimate is that it will cut in half the amount of causalities that die from shock and blood loss on the battlefield.

[7]United States Army Training and Doctrine Command. Annual Report on the Army After Next. (Fort Monroe, VA., 7 December 1998). [Online] Available: www.tradoc.army.mil/dcsdoc/aan.htm, 10 Jan 98, p. 5-6. Strategic preclusion is the idea of moving so fast and with such lethality, that enemies cannot 'set' forces and operate at advantage against us. In the best of cases, this response would be decisive in its own right, settling the issue quickly and with minimal loss of life and property for both sides.

[8]Liddell Hart, John A. English, On Infantry. (New York; Praeger, 1981), 205.

[9]John A. English. On Infantry. (New York; Praeger, 1981), 3.

[10]James R. Fitzsimonds and Jan M Van Tol, "Revolution in Military Affairs," Joint Force Quarterly 4, (Spring 1994): 29.

[11]Ibid. p 29. Taken from Dwight D. Eisenhower, At Ease: Stories I Tell to Friends (New York: Doubleday, 1967), 173.

[12]Sir Basil Henry Liddell Hart, Thoughts on War (London: Faber and Faber, Ltd., 1944.) In Department of the Army, Army Training and Doctrine Command, TRADOC Pamphlet 525-5. Force XXI Operations: A Concept for the Evolution of Full-Dimensional Operations for the Strategic Army of the early Twenty First Century. (Fort Monroe, VA: 1 August 1994.), 1-3.

[13]Christopher Bellamy, <u>The Evolution of Modern Land Warfare. Theory and Practice.</u> (London: Routledge, 1990), 39.

[14]Department of the Army, Army Training and Doctrine Command, TRADOC Pamphlet 525-5, <u>Force XXI Operations: A Concept for the Evolution of Full-Dimensional Operations for the Strategic Army of the early Twenty First Century</u>. (Fort Monroe, VA: 1 August 1994), 43.

[15]Ibid., forward.

[16]Ibid., 2-7.

[17]Ibid., 2-8.

[18]MAJ Jeff Bovais and MAJ Kevin Hyneman, USA, Telephonic Interviews by author, 19 and 21 February 1999. Fort Leavenworth, Kansas. Authors Notes.

[19]MAJ Tony Carbone, USA, Scenario Simulations Office , The Infantry Center, Fort Benning, GA. Telephonic Interview by author, 19 February 1999. Fort Leavenworth, Kansas. Authors Notes. "We model the land Warrior system with mathematical equations. The tests strongly suggest the Land Warrior would greatly increase the lethality of the Infantry Squad and provide them with far better protection."

[20]Bovais, Jeff, MAJ, USA, TSM Soldier, The Infantry Center, Fort Benning, GA. Telephonic Interview by author, 19 February 1999. Fort Leavenworth, Kansas. Authors Notes. The "One Infantry" philosophy is one of the driving forces behind the present model for all Infantry units as a part of Force XXI. As a result the Army is moving to three, nine man infantry squads for all Infantry platoons. The only differences between the platoons will be the weapons squads and the headquarters sections.

[21]Fitzsimonds and Van Tol, 27.

[22]Brian Bond and Martin Alexander, "Liddel Hart and De Gaulle: The doctrines of Limited Liability and Mobile Defense." ed. Peter Paret, <u>Makers of Modern Strategy from Machiavelli to the Nuclear Age</u>. (Princeton, NJ: Princeton University Press, 1986), 623. "The interwar period bears out the Clausewitzian perception that political attitudes, priorities, and constraints exert a dominating influence on the development of armed forces and strategic doctrines." This quote is referencing the cause of the lack of doctrinal and organizational preparation by the French and British in World War II.

[23]Jeff Bovais, "We could use a cell of guys to conduct the research that you are doing up there at Fort Leavenworth."

CHAPTER 2

LITERATURE REVIEW

The purpose of this literature review is to outline the works used to conduct this study. In line with the holistic approach to this paper, it was important to seek information from a variety of sources. These sources include a futuristic perspective on the conduct of warfare as well as a review of the historic conditions that the infantryman in close combat have had to overcome to accomplish his mission as a member of an infantry squad. The historical review also required a detailed inspection of why the US Army Infantry Squad evolved and what factors were considered in determining optimum structure of the Infantry Squad throughout its evolution. The study of the Squad's evolution captured in a variety of sources served to establish the basic evaluation criteria for the future squad. Further, the research for this topic involved a study of current and future technology that could be integrated into consideration for a future Infantry squad. Lastly, to determine the types of forces that the United States Army will have to engage in future conflicts to accomplish national security strategy, the forecasted geostrategic environment was investigated.

The driving force for this literature review was to define criteria that will assist in the development or the future infantry squad. These then were compared to challenges foretold by the effects of time, technology, and contemporary doctrinal military theory. I selected works based on the value they would have on defining the impact on the future infantryman and the most basic army organization, the squad.

The investigation of this topic began long before I set out to write this thesis. The ability of visionaries to fantasize about how future men, adversaries, governments, and the collective body of extraterrestrial beings will settle their differences and provide for their own defense has interested me for some time. It is amazing that authors, such as Orson Wells, could predict the future complexion of combat with remarkable clairvoyance. With dubious knowledge of the technical aspect of how forces operate today, novelists can create surprisingly accurate works. When it comes to prognostication of future warfare, it appears that futurists with a knowledge of technology and its evolution, history, and the world political climate are at an advantage to traditional military theorist. Unbound to parochial opinions on military affairs and doctrine, the civilian author is seemingly less encumbered by the past and is more capable of free thought. During the interwar period of the 1930s and 40s, Liddell Hart acknowledged this fact. He attempted to impress upon his countrymen the importance of vision when attempting to integrate advances in technology into military organizations. He argued that to bring about a change like the one characterized by the revolution in military affairs called blitzkrieg an army must open its mind to new ideas, while avoiding fixation on the past. Thus the real challenge, Hart says is not in planting new ideas into the military mind, but in avoiding parochialism when evolving from the past.[1]

Robert Heinlein's <u>Starship Troopers</u> epitomizes the essence of the works that offered unique perceptive on what the uncertain future might hold for the infantry soldier and squad. This novel depicted how the future mobile infantry (MI) would play an integral part in the defense of the earth, despite the abundance of high tech weapons available for its protection from alien creatures. In <u>Starship Troopers</u> Heinlein describes

17

the composition of the MI. The standard MI soldier is extremely physically and mentally fit and is tested and evaluated in a challenging basic training environment. The soldier wears a powered suit into combat that allows him to fight with an extraordinary amount of armament and equipment. The suit also offers him the ability to maneuver at incredible speeds. The MI moves to the point of decision by future spacecraft. Once in the objective area, these troopers conduct a futuristic airborne insertion through the target planet's atmosphere. The interaction between the MI squad on the ground showed a striking resemblance today's infantry squads.

Heinlein envisions future combat conducted by the MI, the elite and major arm of earth's defense forces, that is similar to the close combat fought in the twentieth century. In his story Earth's forces choose to fight with the MI to avoid mass destruction of the planets they invade and to fight the enemy where he lives which requires infantry type forces. The story emphasizes the importance of being physically and mentally trained and conditioned for the stresses of combat. During the time he published the book military nuclear theory dominated thought. He tried to emphasis by his predominant theme the importance of the squad's ability to fight as a unit and the individual worth of each soldier. This future perspective of combat, grounded in the present day combat principles of hard training and close combat, inspired me to "think outside of the box,"[2] with respect to what might be for the infantryman.

The review of historic books and literature provided invaluable information about the development of the United States Army Infantry squad, the face of battle and the effect infantry has had on war through the ages and vice versa.

A review of government publications, such as Virgil Ney's <u>Organization and Equipment of the Infantry Rifle Squad: From Valley Forge to R.O.A.D.</u> (Re-Organization of the Army Division), were invaluable sources of information. These documents illustrated the genesis and evolution of the squad organization in infantry units throughout the Army's modern history. This study researched all of the major US Army experiments and tests that the Infantry Branch used to analyze the optimum squad structure. Perhaps the most important aspect of this literature review was the discovery of the lessons learned from major conflicts and then how the testing bodies incorporated them into squad evaluation and testing. In each experiment, the testing bodies wrote a summary of their testing philosophy and testing results and recommendations. The recommendations that accompanied the squad structural proposals, outlined the selection criteria used in each test as it related to the squad of the times. In most cases, the selection criteria were based on the combat experience of the authors gained from the recent conflicts. The power of this research rests in the review of each experiment's criteria for forming a squad organization. These insights allowed the use of past selection criteria as a basis to nominate a future squad organization.

Other significant works of history offered proof of the relevance of the infantry squad as an organization throughout the evolution of warfare. <u>On Infantry</u> by John English outlines a comprehensive history of the infantry organization from a plethora of perspectives. English's work considers infantry units from all major armies since the 1800s. He defines the infantry as a force from the formation of the squad as a tool to decentralize major units of battalion size on the battlefield for survivability reasons. He also sheds light on how the infantry remained relevant throughout time despite many

Revolutions in Military Affairs that threatened to reduce or remove the significance of the Infantry in maneuver warfare in each modern era.

I also explored works by the preeminent thinkers and writers on the face of battle. S. L. A. Marshall's Men Against Fire offered observations on methods for success in battle at the small unit level. Marshall used evidence from combat observations and interviews to argue for established criteria for infantry squads and fighting organizations. Marshall's perspective gives a unique account of combat not jaded by parochialism, that can sometimes fill Department of Defense research or Army test results. These works offer principles for squad selection criteria that are timeless.

To forecast the future challenges for the infantry squad of the next millennium, I explored the Department of Defense and the Army's emerging doctrine. Two sources were vital to this research, TRADOC Pamphlet 525-5, Force XXI Operations: A Concept for the Evolution of Full-Dimensional Operations for the Strategic Army of the early Twenty First Century, and The Annual Report on The Army After Next Project to the Chief of Staff of the Army. TRADOC Pamphlet 525-5, is the driving force behind the Army's organization and doctrinal development. It integrates current emerging threat and technology considerations and drives the development of Army doctrine for the first ten to fifteen years of the twenty-first century. TRADOC Pamphlet 525-5 makes an argument for the necessary applications of technology and organizational changes that must occur now to meet emerging contemporary challenges. The Army After Next (AAN) doctrine, based on the Department of Defense's Joint Vision XXI, strives to focus the development of the Army after the year 2015. AAN is a well-written futuristic vision that provides the Army theorists and developers guidance and direction for force development. It systematically explores and defines the future threat to national security and then offers solutions for shaping the force and driving technological development. It aptly states that, "Forecasting tomorrow's geostrategic environment forms the first step in any investigation into future warfare."[3]

TRADOC tested the AAN theories in a series of futuristic war games. To conduct the AAN series of war games, TRADOC brought civilian technological experts and DOD intelligence and operations personnel together to form a thinking enemy for the simulations. The games provided the US force with realistic futuristic capabilities. This force dominated the opposition in technology applications and information processing. The war games results shape the recommendations for future research and doctrinal solutions advocated by AAN and give it validity. The AAN theory takes all that is good about-unconstrained futurist thinking and melds it with realistic future constraints and conditions of technology and threat.

Contemporary authors that forecast the future geostrategic environment offered a perspective about the future threat and physical environment that the Infantry squad of year 2015 and beyond will fight. Robert D Kaplin's article, "The Coming Anarchy," defines the impacts of the current world situation coupled with increased population and a depletion of natural resources and what that holds for the world human population. Although Kaplin's thesis describes "dooms day" type conditions, it sheds light on the complexion of our nation's and thus the infantry's future adversaries. These prognostications, again grounded in fact and statistical trends, offer other possibilities of qualities the infantry squad must possess, and thus refine and verify selection criteria for the squad.

The Infantry School and the TRADOC system manager soldier, have been generous in providing technological data and experimental findings on the development of new infantry-based systems. This research, the majority of which was conducted over the Internet and telephone, allowed an established a baseline for technology available now and for what is possible by the year 2015. Although the documents were not entirely comprehensive, they collectively provide an extensive amount of data and equipment specifications that could collate into future forms. The technology development study also set limitations on how far into the future I was able to evaluate the future squad. Adherence to the time limitations of this type of realistic study agrees with the philosophy captured in a passage from the AAN doctrine. It states, "First, every revolution, whether political, economic, or military, unfolds in evolutionary steps. [TRADOC Pam 525-5 states that it generally takes at least half a generation, or about 15 years] for vision and ideas to mature into secure and irreversible change. [In the army] it takes about that long to grow a battalion commander or platoon sergeant or to develop, test and field major systems."[4]

I completed my literature review with exploration of the simulation research and mathematically modeling on the land warrior system under development at the Infantry School. I conducted this research on the findings of the Fort Benning Simulation Center by conducting telephone interviews and from raw data from test results published in non-classified documents. I also examined the empirical data and findings of mathematical models used to evaluate the Land Warrior System. From this research, I was able to determine the performance capabilities of the advanced systems, as well as, the demonstrated capabilities and deficiencies identified during actual field testing.

[1]Sir Basil Henry Liddell Hart, <u>Thoughts on War</u> (London: Faber and Faber, Ltd., 1944). From TRADOC manual 525-5, 1-3.

[2]"Thinking outside of the box" is an often and overused expression at the United States Command and General Staff College, which translates into one's ability to resist the confines of traditional thoughts and ideas, in an attempt to think for oneself.

[3]United States Army Training and Doctrine Command. <u>Annual Report on the Army After Next</u>. (Fort Monroe, VA: 7 December 1998). [Online] available at http://www.tradoc.army.mil/dcsdoc/aan.htm, accessed 20 January 1999, 1.

[4]LTC John Medve, USA. <u>Knowledge and Speed: The Annual Report on The Army After Next Project to the Chief of Staff of the Army.</u> (Fort Monroe, VA: 1 August 1997), 3.

CHAPTER 3

RESEARCH METHODOLOGY

For this thesis, a variety of sources will be used to establish selection criteria for the composition of the future infantry squad. The significance of the thesis is not necessarily the findings or recommendation for composition, but is the process and considerations for development of the squad organization. It was imperative to make this a holistic approach. The detailed research was used in many instances to substantiate a point, rather than simply enumerate findings. This allowed the incorporation of many unique aspects of the research question that have been explored by many others at great length.

The review began with the evolution of the United States Army infantry squad organization from its modern beginnings to the present day structure. The significance of this research lays in a review of why the squad evolved and how the experimentation and research teams involved in the various studies conducted their tests. The investigation revealed that failures or inadequacies of the organization identified in a major conflict such as, World War II, Korea, and Vietnam, precipitated most of the organizational changes to the squad. From this study, certain qualities that appear inalienable to the squad were extrapolated. These qualities remain consistent through time because the essence of the squad is the soldiers that serve in it. Thus the capacity of the human brain and the physiological composition of man, even with the addition of high-tech gadgetry bound its capabilities.

A review of the complexion of combat and its impact on units and individuals broadened the study's perspective of the squad's growth. History offers perspectives from other military theorists and illustrates the effect of combat on men, units, and military organizations in general. History also measures successes and failure along less subjective terms than the squad experimentation studies that offer many biases. It also offers the clairvoyance that hindsight allows. The study of history shows how nations and armies have dealt with the occurrences of things, such as a Revolution in Military Affairs, and shows how they have responded to them. The history study allowed parallels to be drawn to future squad structure, and the net result was to further reinforce the basic selection criteria for the squad drawn from the squad history study.

Perhaps one of the most important research areas for this study is the examination of the technology available for application into the future infantry squad. It is significant to note that this examination considered not only current developmental projects but also cutting edge technology that could feasibly impact on the squad's capabilities and composition. From the infantryman's perspective, the traditional problem with technological innovations that allow the infantryman to become more lethal results in an increase to the soldier's load. As the Army tries to improve the efficiency of the infantry, it overburdens the members of the organization with unmanageable weight. A quote from General Hartzog, former commander of the United States Training and Doctrine Command, captures the essence of this oxymoron. He says, "Today we are very close to being overcome by a bow-wave of new and increasingly sophisticated technology.... Some good ideas just aren't. If technology is to be truly useful it must enable, not encumber, our people."[1] Using this perspective and by being in a safe place to ponder such options, I could shape the infantryman as a component of the squad from the ground up. Besides allowing me to apply the ideal equipment onto the infantryman, the study of technology allows me to further scrutinize the effective squad qualities and capabilities.

To examine the current infantry equipment developments I collected information from the TRADOC System Manager Solider (TSM Soldier), the Fort Benning Simulations Center, and Officers involved with the field testing at Fort Bragg and the AWE at the National Training Center. Representatives from Project Manager Soldier (PM soldier) at Fort Belvoir, Virginia, provided all the current publications of the Special Text series to develop the Land Warrior Project for review. Lastly, I explored the data published by Natick Research, Development, and Engineering Center Laboratories, on the simulations conducted by them on the Land Warrior System and how it affected the factors of lethality, suppression, target detection, and other qualities.

To identify the operating conditions that the infantry squad of 2015 will operate, it is imperative to examine the future threats to U.S. national security. This analysis will dictate the types of future threat the United States Army will face and may suggest how it will have to fight to win the nations future battles. Accuracy in predicting the future serves the military theorists well. If the Army can properly forecast what its force must do to win then the force structure created will properly function in the future environment and have the ability to respond to potential threats. As the Army After Next doctrine points out, "Forecasting tomorrow's geostrategic environment forms the first step in any investigation into future warfare."[2] To compound the problem in today's world, it is clear that the future threat is unclear. As TRADOC's Force XXI guidance states, "The days of the all-purpose doctrinal threat template are gone, just as the days of a single-prescription Army doctrine are gone."[3] Understanding the forecasted geostrategic

environment will allow me to further refine the basic squad qualities being examined.

TRADOC has published several works on their vision of future doctrine.

TRADOC's vision provides guidance for future force development in all areas from

logistics to small unit tactics and training. These publications by TRADOC form the

basis for realistic future thought on the structure and role of the infantry squad. To

continue to dominate as a world power well into the twenty-first century, the Army

recognized the need to evaluate its direction and future development. To guide the Army,

TRADOC produced several documents to espouse the vision and direction the Army

would take to remain relevant after the Gulf War. The Army After Next manuals

published annually and the Force XXI publication TRADOC Pamphlet 525-5, Force XXI

Operations: A Concept for the Evolution of Full-Dimensional Operations for the

Strategic Army of the early Twenty First Century published in 1994, describes why and

how the Army must evolve. TRADOC's future doctrine outlines the operational

framework for the force. Army Force XXI doctrine indeed advocates the relevance of

ground forces and particular small units. TRADOC Pamphlet 525-5 states, "In a strategic

environment without a single pervasive threat, the utility of land forces for control to gain

strategic aims increases. Control is an end state."[4] The TRADOC commander's vision,

which is based on guidance from Joint Vision 2010 and on their own perception of future

operations, will enable me to further refine the criteria for selecting a future squad.

In summation, I will equate criteria found and identified by the above factors to

advocate a squad structure of the future and form my conclusion. Along with my vision of the future squad, I will recommend contemporary considerations and identify areas for

future research.

---

[1]GEN William W. Hartzog. USA, <u>Land Combat in the 21st Century</u>, (Fort Monroe, VA: United States Army Training and Doctrine Command, 1994) [Online] Available http://www.monroe.army.mil/cmdpubs/landcmbt.htm, accessed 10 June 1998, 3.

[2]<u>Annual Report on the Army After Next</u>. (Fort Monroe, VA: United States Army Training and Doctrine Command, 7 December 1998), [Online] Available www.tradoc.army.mil/dcsdoc/aan.htm. accessed 15 January 1999, 1.

[3]Department of the Army, TRADOC Pamphlet 525-5. <u>Force XXI Operations: A Concept for the Evolution of Full-Dimensional Operations for the Strategic Army of the early Twenty-First Century</u>. (Fort Monroe, VA: United States Army Training and Doctrine Command, 1 August 1994), 2-11.

[4]Ibid., 3-22.

CHAPTER 4

ANALYSIS

Squad Evolution

The squad as it is known today, is essentially an
American military development.[1]

The library is full of scholarly works about the evolution and the development of

the infantry squad. The preponderance of studies lack detailed assessment of the squads

operating environment. The studies also lack vision describing or prescribing what form

the squad should take to remain relevant for the future. Most works discuss how the

Army could make the squad a better and more efficient organization, but fail to

incorporate why. Military theorists face a logic problem. They attempt to pattern combat

after the war most recently fought and create organizations that fight the model for

success in the last war, not the one they will fight in the future. This thesis will attempt

to find a solution.

In the later stages of the American Civil War, Major General Emory Upton, who

later wrote America's first modern tactical battle drills, officially developed the first

tactical infantry squads for the United States Army. The eight-man squad served as a

basis for developing technical proficiency and tactical employment and also provided

social identity for the members of the organization. During the Civil War as early as 1863

the Army recognized that soldiers needed to bond with each other in a formal close-knit

organization. The squad offered a solution to the problem.[2]

As stated in the opening quote, the modern infantry squad, is essentially an

American development.[3] The evolution of the squad as an independent operating tactical entity emerged during the United States westward expansion. A guerilla force, the American Indians, presented unique challenges to America's frontier army in a new combat environment. To defeat the Indians, the Army was forced to conduct combat operations in a decentralized manner over huge expanses of terrain. Thus, to win, small tactical units adapted and ably conducted decentralized operations that the Army might be familiar with today. Unfortunately, the stalking, scouting, and movement techniques used to defeat the Indians in close combat were lost by the soldier and the Army until World War II. The Army failed to apply the lessons learned on the frontier due to the perceived dominance of modern artillery and by a failure to capture the tactical successes in the West. As a result, the squad lost its identity in the quagmire of attrition warfare in World War I.[4] World War I warfare again defined the squad as an administrative body rather than a tactical entity. The Army's emphasis shifted from training squads for maneuver to training specialists that platoons could distribute throughout their front to meet their objectives. Thus, the Army discounted the squad as a tactical entity. Sections of hand bombers and riflemen replaced the tactical squad organization that had developed on the American Frontier.[5]

The infantry squad developed because of an identified need to adequately control individuals on the industrial age battlefield that increasingly called for dispersion for survival. Commanders without effectively organized small tactical units found it challenging to maintain control to effectively mass forces and fires in combat.[6] The solution to this problem was the development of the squad as the basic tactical unit on the battlefield. When the American military squad began to evolve the Army defined it as, "The smallest unit to conduct tactical operations under command of its own leader."[7] It

30

was further defined in the Dictionary of U.S. Army Terms in 1946 as, "A Group of enlisted men organized as a team; smallest tactical unit consisting of only as many men as [one] leader can directly control."[8]

This thesis begins with examination of the squad in the midst of the first major RMA in this century that occurred during the beginning of World War II. Since the Great War the term "squad" has personified the essence of the infantry. To anyone familiar with the profession of arms, the term squad describes a small group of men equipped with small arms and led by a noncommissioned officer (NCO). The members of the squad have an image that says they are self-reliant, tough soldiers who can do more with their hands and weapons then most normal men. Together, these men form the squad. The men of the squad fight the wars and the squad can be considered the touchstone of the Army.

In 1940, the Army identified the requirement of a squad to function as an independent unit that could provide independent fire and movement for the Infantry rifle platoon and this caused the squad to change. The Army found new purpose for the traditional eight-man squad of the 1870s, which was created for combat but now used almost exclusively for administrative control of soldiers. Uptons's squad lasted nearly eighty years, from the late 1860s until 1940, when it was reorganized into a twelve-man, three-team organization. Tactical control of the men under fire was the primary reason identified for changing the organization, thus the Army allowed for a corporal assistant squad leader to direct the fire of the automatic rifle team which manned the BAR (M 1918A2). Squad designers also sought to improve the firepower and resiliency that were remedied by larger squad size.

31

In the after-action reviews from World War II, in the Report of Activities, Army Field Forces, 1945-1949, the Army recognized that the 12-man squad was too big for one leader to control. The report pointed out that in combat one man could not lead or directly manage more than eight-men at a time.[9] Findings also showed that greater weapons lethality of the modern age made it imperative to increase the dispersion of the force. Wanting more dispersion for protection and a more favorable leader to led ratio; they advocated the adoption of a squad no larger than nine men.

Based on the findings from the Report of Committee "B" on Tactics and Techniques, published for the leaders at the Infantry Conference of 1946, the Army changed the infantry squad and officially transformed it into a nine-man organization led by a squad leader and assistant squad leader. Although they reorganized the squad, many leaders were not satisfied that the squad so structured would serve as an capable independent organization. One Infantry Conference Committee felt the nine-man squad was too small to effectively conduct fire and maneuver and should perform tasks as a part of platoon operations in either fire or maneuver.[10]

Infantry units fought during the Korean War with the nine-man squad organization authorized by the Table of Organization and Equipment (TOE). As a result of that war, many observations surfaced about the psychological and physical conditioning required to function as a member of a squad. The United States Continental Army authored A Study of the Infantry Rifle Squad (ASIRS) TOE in 1956, which examined the perceived deficiencies of the nine-man infantry squad after the Korean War. To the panel, it was apparent that the design of the squad and its inability to conduct fire and maneuver was detrimental to the infantry platoon and company organization. Leaders at

32

the 1956 Infantry Conference agreed that, one squad with one leader could not support itself with a base of fire and maneuver.[11] Further, the study found that the leader-to-led ratio should be no greater than five to one, and that the squad must be able to absorb 25 percent causalities and still function as designed.[12] The ASIRS Report also advocated that the squad have two balanced teams led by sergeants and that each team should possess an automatic weapon. This balanced team concept would allow either team to provide suppression in the fire role, or maneuver when called upon.[13] The qualities desired were increased firepower, a favorable leader to led ratio, and resiliency.

The ASIRS Study was conducted as a part of the Reorganization of the Current Infantry Division (ROCID). The ROCID was an initiative designed to modernize the infantry after the Korean War. It was also a part of the Army's Pentomic reorganization.[14] Thus, under the provisions of TO&E 17-17T ROICD, the Army created the eleven-man, two fire team squad in December of 1956.

In 1961, the Army conducted another comprehensive organizational study of the infantry squad. The United States Army Combat Development Center (CDEC) orchestrated the study. As a result, the CDEC sponsored two field studies. The first was conducted at Fort Ord, California, named the Optimum Composition of the Rifle Squad and Platoon (OCRSP), and involved extensive field testing and the evaluation of empirical data. The other study the Rifle Squad and Platoon Evaluation Program (RSPEP) conducted at Fort Benning was mainly a cerebral exercise that involved no troop maneuver exercises.

The Fort Ord OCRSP study physically experimented with a variety of different sized infantry squads with multiple internal leadership and organizational structures. It

33

also incorporated facts gained from interviews with combat veterans from World War II and Korea. The OCRSP choose nine evaluation criteria. They were: leadership, control, maneuverability under fire, flexibility in structure, firepower, mobility, logistics, tactical capabilities, and staying power. The purpose of this experiment was to discover what effect the introduction of new weapon systems, namely the M14 that would replace the M1, the M60 machine gun that would replace the BAR, and the M79 grenade launcher, would have on the squad. Also the study aimed at objectively defining the optimal squad organization equipped with the new weapons.[15]

The OCRSP found that an eleven-man squad organized with two five-man fire teams led by NCOs was the optimal design. The committee, composed of combat veterans from Korea, felt that the squad needed eleven men in order to dominate the fight in close terrain. They also concluded that the eleven-man squad was a good balance between maneuverability (more teams or people being harder to maneuver) and staying power (the ability to absorb and take care of causalities and still function as designed). Additionally, the study proved that the squad lost the ability to fire and maneuver when its strength dropped somewhere between seven to eight men. The veterans on the test panel emphatically advocated the use of the M-60 style machine gun in the squad organization to give it adequate firepower. And although it was eleven pounds heavier than the BAR, they advocated that each fire team should have an organic M-60 machine gun. Lastly, the study identified sustainability (staying power or resiliency) and lethality as the most important qualities for the squad.[16]

The CDEC supervised the RSPEP at Fort Benning mainly to evaluate the utility of adding the M-60 machine gun to the infantry squad. But, RSPEP goals also included determination of assignment of the M79 grenade launcher to the squad and whether to keep the balanced fire team concept. Its last goal was to optimize the leader-to-led ratio within the squad.

As a result of the experiment, the CDEC for the first time formally defined the fire team as "a groupment of individuals and weapons, in either a balanced or unbalanced configuration, each of which can function as the base of fire or maneuver element."[17] It also defined staying power as "the built-in capability of a unit to sustain itself in combat."[18] Then further qualified it by stating, "staying power is measured in terms of the length of time a unit can remain combat effective despite battle attrition."[19]

The RSPEP advocated a ten-man squad organized into two fire teams, one fire team with four men and one fire team with five men. The difference in the CDEC study was that the RSPEP espoused that the unbalanced teams would increase flexibility. It should be noted the Fort Benning study contained no objective data and was subjective in nature. It failed to incorporate the findings from the live simulations conducted at Fort Ord during the OCRSP. The failure to adopt the recommendation by the OCRSP experiments conducted at Fort Ord which advocating an eleven-man squad was probably impacted more by cost than anything else.[20]

Although the Infantry School concurred with the findings of the CDEC in its initial OCRSP study, it was forced to reduce the number of men in a squad to ten, in order facilitate the increase in the number of active army divisions from fourteen to sixteen in January 1962. Thus, it accepted the recommendation from the RSPEP Study. The Reorganization of the Active Army Division (ROAD) dictated via T/O & E 7-18E,[21] the infantry squad would become a ten-man organization with organic five- and four-man fire teams all equipped with M-14s. The M-14 would serve as both the rifleman's and automatic rifleman's weapon, the later equipped with bipod. The Army used this organization to fight the Vietnam War.

The United States Army Combat Developments Command (CDC) captured the opinions of the combat infantrymen in Vietnam and the veterans that returned home during the war. The CDC asked twenty-five questions which pertained to "weapons, organization, personnel, communications, firepower, controllability and tactics."[22] The 509 infantrymen surveyed rendered the following opinions. First, the optimum squad organization consists of two fire teams led by a squad leader and two team leaders. Next, 90 percent of those surveyed said that the 11-man squad was the optimal size. Additionally, the combat infantrymen said the M-60 was too hard to control when attached to a squad and that a lightweight automatic weapon was needed to achieve adequate suppression. Lastly, to assist with controllability, 65 percent of the men noted that team leaders should have radios to talk with their squad leaders.[23]

From the CDC survey, the Army initiated the first Infantry Rifle Unit Study (IRUS), published in 1969, to evaluate the optimal composition of the infantry squad. They choose the following evaluation and selection criteria: controllability, maneuverability, survivability, sustainability, intelligence and counterintelligence, and fire effectiveness. The test evaluated the organizations using live simulations for squads ranging in size from seven to sixteen men. They also experimented with the new weapons of the time, the M-16 rifle and the M-63A light machine gun.[24]

The findings of the IRUS were that once the squad fell to below nine men it lost its ability to simultaneously conduct fire and maneuver. It judged the eleven-man squad with two balanced fire teams as the optimal composition for the organization. The findings of the study also stipulated that team leaders should have radios.[25]

The next IRUS study, again sponsored by the CDC, and published in 1975 advocated an eleven-man squad with two five-man fire teams led by NCOs. This study used the same evaluation criteria as the first IRUS study, save the fire effectiveness factor. This unique study focused on the physiological factors of physical stress, effects of attrition, and advantages of intra squad communication.[26] The CDC found results that resembled the results of the earlier study published in 1969. The design authors made significant gains during this study by using an ARTEP style of grade sheet. Further, they considered the human aspect of the infantryman and how he individually impacted on the squad.[27]

As the Cold War raged in the seventies and eighties, the United States Army morphed the infantry squad to fit into the modern form of infantry conveyance. Units that owned the M-113 Armored Personnel Carrier (APC) were not authorized additional soldiers to drive the vehicle or man the .50 caliber machine gun. Thus, by default, the eleven-man squad became a nine-man dismounted element in all the mechanized units. General Wickham's Army of Excellence (AOE) army force design enhanced the deployability of the light force divisions. The administration's goal enumerated by the Division 84 Model called for the entire light division to fly to a point of entry with 500 C-141 sorties. To reduce the number in the division from 14,000 to 10,700 men the Army adopted a nine-man squad organization. The AOEs also established a goal, "To standardize the infantry squad in all division structures". Next the Army designed the Bradley Fighting Vehicle to carry only two nine-man dismounted squads.[28]

As technology and modernization have progressed, the Army has divorced itself from the knowledge, experience, and testing that it conducted on the matter of squad composition. The 11-man squad died because the Army designed airframes and armored fighting vehicles that would not accommodate its size, not because of its inability to operate on the modern battlefield. Further, the Army has suffered from a distinct lack of adequate field testing to validate the optimum size of the squad since the Vietnam War.

In the quest for establishing the optimum squad composition for the year 2015, it is important to summarize the selection criteria used by past war fighters to judge the squad. Over decades of research, the qualities consistently chosen to evaluate the squad were: dispersion, control in contact, leader-to-led ratio, maneuverability under fire (the ability to fire and maneuver), logistics (the ability to sustain itself in the field by what it could carry by itself), resiliency (the ability to squad to handle combat losses and continue to function as it was designed), and lethality (the amount of fire that could be brought to bare on the enemy).

Effects of Information Age Technology

Henry Ford never met Heinz Guderian, the German General commonly held most responsible for exploiting Ford's invention to gain victory on the battlefield. Likewise, history will eventually produce the warrior who will capitalize on the opportunities offered by Bill Gates and the revolution most often associated with his name.[29]

Army After Next

Since the beginning of time, man has sought better ways to kill his fellow man in war. Through mostly civilian-oriented scientific exploration with the purpose of making life better for mankind, man has adapted science and applied it to the battlefield. Toffeler argues that nations make war by the same means that they make money. This is the logical extension of the use of technology or the tools on hand. Man can easily alter the technology used by a nation perfected to efficiently produce durable goods and capital to feed people, into military defense applications. Thus the nations that build state-of-the-art machines to earn capital are at a great advantage when it comes to building war machines.[30]

Although nations can apply raw industrial technological advances into applied weapons relatively quickly, it is difficult to rapidly integrate them directly into military systems of worth. Christopher Bellamy, author of the book The Evolution of Modern Land Warfare: Theory and Practice, understood this phenomenon. He wrote, "There has usually been a time lag between the idea for a new weapon or other revolutionary technological advance, its appearance and limited adoption and its assimilation into the conduct of warfare through new tactical, operational and strategic forms."[31]

In broad terms, force developers try to rush new technology into the hands of soldiers to meet certain objectives. Generally technicians think a quicker solution will be a better solution when it comes to technological development. But to adapt effective systems designers must consider how technology can best be applied to the soldier before thrusting into his hands. The 75th Ranger Regiment has the funds to purchase the minor pieces of equipment it deems necessary to accomplish its mission. When asked by several NCOs why the Rangers did not immediately go out and buy the civilian equipment they felt that they needed without waiting for a bureaucrat to test it, Colonel McChrystal, the 75th Ranger Regimental Commander stated, "Because the Ranger warehouse is full of good ideas not being used and I don't want to add to it when you figure out what I bought you doesn't work." Bellamy also stated, "Technology must match man: man is the measure.... Throughout the history of warfare ... technology and man have always striven for harmony, and man has imposed his limitations on technology."[32] Man's capacity to think and react impose limitations on technology applications for combat. As long as man is in the loop and robotic systems cannot independently operate, then man's intelligence capacity and physiology will continue to drive technological applications.[33]

In modern terms, the first large technological disparity for the infantry in general was the introduction of the French Chassepot rifle with a range of 2,000 yards against the German Needle Gun sighted to about 600 yards. Quantifiably this is when "masses of manpower had, in fact, surrendered its position of superiority on the field of battle to concentrated firepower."[34] Although they did not fully understand it, soldiers began to subscribe to the "Theory of the Rigid, Constant Come of Misses." Though most soldiers did not understand it, they respected the beaten zone, and it soon became known as no mans land. Further they appreciated that it extended out to the effective range of the enemies weapon systems, all of which created a dominance of the defensive form of maneuver.[35]

As the lethality of weapons on the battlefield increased, men began to disperse for protection. Soldiers also saw that it was advantages to use the shovel to sink below the earth for protection. Thus enemy soldiers became increasingly more difficult to detect, acquire, and engage. This phenomenon created a condition described as the disappearing battlefield and attributed to making the defense the dominant form of battle at the turn of the nineteenth century.[36]

As technology increased, lethality followed suit especially for high-tech systems like the plane. In World War II, it took 9,070 bombs dropped by an armada of B-17s to ensure a 90 percent probability of kill (PK) against a single 60-foot by 100- foot building. By the time of the Vietnam conflict, 175 bombs were required. Today, it takes only one precision-guided bomb to achieve the same PK.[37] The same seems to hold true for other sophisticated weapons, such as antitank systems, "In World War II an average of eighteen rounds were needed to kill a tank at a range of 800 yards, during the 1973 Arab-Israeli War the average was two rounds at 1200 yards, and by Desert Storm one round at 2400 yards."[38] Paradoxically, as the technical evolution has progressed the predominant infantry weapons have not followed the same pattern illustrated above. "In Napoleonic battles, it was calculated that about three to five hundred shots had to be fired for each hit on an enemy soldier, whereas in the Manchurian war the number was nearer 20,000 shots and in Vietnam around 600,000."[39] This increase in rounds to destroy a target leads to the conclusion that technology has not had as big an impact on the infantry as it has the other Army branches and services.

The United States has often used technology as the panacea for all military problems. This attitude attributed to the Allied shortage of infantry in World War II, which "lie[s] in a decided Anglo-Saxon preference for technological solutions and the somewhat related pursuit of a high standard of living both on and off the battlefield."[40] History shows that technology developers in their zeal to perfect their systems sometimes may go too far. The production of the German MG 34 machine gun criticized for a high jamming and malfunction rate illustrates this point. "As weapons go, the MG 34 demonstrated craftsmanship of the highest order, and its milled components necessitated very fine tolerances--a veritable work of art. Unfortunately, works of art are usually expensive and not created for fellows to drag about through mud, dust, snow, and sand."[41]

"Since the beginning of the industrial age, technological warfare--the applied science of killing--has eclipsed all other dynamics of change. For many, this magnitude and newness of science, threatens the reliability of precedent as a useful mechanism for predicting the course of war."[42] This uncertainty can be supported by this statement from Lieutenant Colonel John Medve who says, "Ironically, success in the first major war of the Atomic Age hinged not on high technology but on the performance of the old-fashioned soldier on foot, the ancient and unglamorous 'Cinderella' of the Army."[43] Furthermore, after a study of the thirty major military engagements since World War II it is important to note that infantry has played a vital if not dominant role in all the outcomes.[44]

With this infantry dominance on the battlefield as a theme, it would behoove any force to strive for improvements to the Infantry system as an integral part of the modern combat team development. The Army could view the infantryman from a utilitarian perspective as a weapons platform. Paradoxically, the trend above would lead the military to strap new technology to a soldier's back to improve his lethality, when really the military run the risk of reducing his potential on the battlefield by destroying his mobility. TRADOC Pamphlet 525-5 defines the imperative: "Dismounted force mobility and maneuver improvements will be achieved by lightening the soldier's load, increasing his ability to overcome terrain and obstacle restrictions, optimizing the performance of his equipment, and improving his physiology."[45] Until we develop powered suits to make the infantryman capable of maneuvering with significant ease, we have to make his equipment as light and as lethal as possible. There has traditionally been an inverse relationship between lethality and equipment weight. As Chris Yangiger, a civilian military systems designer from the AAI Corporation advocates, "The goal is [to develop] items that will be useful and practical to the individual soldier.... We need to design things that reduce battle fatigue, improve effectiveness and communications...."[46]

It is important to reiterate what General Hartzog, a former Commander TRADOC said about technology. As quoted earlier, General Hartzog believed that technology should not be used for its own sake. To be used the systems be ergonomically designed and enhance the soldiers ability to do his job.[47] We must apply General Hartzog's theme into the application of technology to fashion useable items for the Infantryman's use. We possess the potential to increase the lethality and effectiveness of the individual soldier. Properly suited the squad will again match up well against armor. As John English stated, "Technological improvements in his weapons inventory have made the man fighting on foot a more dangerous adversary than ever before. The smallest target and most universally mobile of all weapons carriers, the foot infantryman with his 'computer-brain' has proved a tougher species than Fuller ever imagined him."[48]

Information age technology holds still untapped mysteries to the discovery of Star Trek vintage weapon systems. New or exotic weapons, as Micheal Mazarr refers to them in his article, "The Military Technical Revolution, A Structural Framework," are still fifteen years away from serious testing and development. Additionally, Mazarr says the impact of lasers and particle beam weapons may be hard to predict.[49] The concentration of effort is on leveraging the technology of the information age to enable soldiers in the foreseeable future. According to AAN doctrine, microchip applications will enable all members of the force to have a relevant common picture of the battlefield and use that knowledge to move quicker than the enemy. This information dominance will enable our forces to maneuver around enemy troop concentrations and arrive at the decisive point while avoiding losses to men and equipment. This relative common picture also makes the infantryman the ideal mobile sensor. The Infantry squad has the ability to move quietly into enemy terrain and can relay accurate enemy information to a land-, sea- or air-based shooter in all-weather conditions.

With huge advances in data processing and information transmission, the soldier is stilled hampered by the weight of energy storage systems. Energy technician's exploration in alternate power sources and decreased power requirements for modern systems will have immediate impact on the foot soldier. The weight of conventional batteries to power communication and information systems presently over burdened the Infantry squad. Technology advances in power storage and hybrid power sources hold the answers to questions that must be answered before production of sophisticated powerful computer based systems can continue for the soldier.

Medical advances will also improve the sustainment potential for the Infantry Squad. The Army has developed the 911 bandage, which is a self-contained, self-sealing bandage and or trauma kit, that contains antibiotics, blood coagulants, and painkiller. A soldier can apply this bandage to himself or his buddy and it will sustain life ten times better than the old bandages. This system allows soldiers to administer effective life-sustaining first aid to each other at the point of injury and promises to decrease mortality rates.[50]

Land Warrior

Today's developments in technology for infantry applications indeed reflect the growth in the nation's information age technology. TRADOC's land warrior (LW) system design leverages the advantages offered by communications and information technologies that are common in every home and business in America. The land warrior integrates the soldier into the Army's Force XXI architecture, by making him a part of the relevant common picture. With the land warrior system, the infantryman will continuously feed his location and enemy situation reports into the force's database of which everyone has access. Additionally, infantry forces can draw from the information in the same database to digitally paint his area of operations on his heads-up display indicating locations of all local friendly and enemy units.

The LW places the soldier at the heart of the system. Designers fabricate all components ergonomically to fit the soldier. The system provides each soldier with an improved ballistic integrated helmet, which houses the heads-up display, passive night vision device, earpiece and boom microphone for the intersquad radio. Each soldier will wear a load-bearing vest (LBV) which houses the LW computer with GPS, individual radio, battery pack, improved body armor, and traditional sustainment equipment. Project managers have designed the traditional load bearing equipment to include storage for ammunition, water, bayonet, and food.

The LW will carry the M4 Carbine with the Special Operations Modification (SOP MOD) kit. The SOP MOD kit includes a passive laser-aiming light or leader illuminator, a tactical flashlight, and a close combat optic. The Thermal Weapon Sight (TWS) with video camera mounts on top of the M4 to integrate the weapon sites with the

(TWS) with video camera mounts on top of the M4 to integrate the weapon sites with the computer heads-up display and target designator. Embedded in the TWS system is a camera for recording real-time digital footage, a laser-range finder, and a compass which can be read by the soldier using the heads-up display.

The LW communications system allows the soldier to speak to and hear every member of the squad, via internal inter-squad radio. This lightweight radio is integrated into the helmet and offers hands off communications. The squad leader is equipped with an additional radio to speak with the platoon leader, which is also integrated into the helmet.

The LW computer integrates the infantryman into the force electronically and affords each soldier the ability to operate as a part of the digital force. The LW computer receives and processes data similar to any personal computer. Commanders can instantaneously send operations orders and fragmentary orders to any soldier or leader on the battlefield. An embedded software pack provides the ability to load and process digital maps and graphics as well. Unique individual software packages also provide the soldier and the leader checklists designed to improve troop-leading procedures. The LW leaders have a remote keyboard that allows for rapid word processing, digital communications, and transmission of situational reports to higher and adjacent units. The computer also facilitates sending visual images over the radio to higher headquarters for reconnaissance as well as targeting information to improve the infantryman's ability to serve as a sensor in the sensor-to-shooter link.

The integrated GPS transmits periodic signals to the force over a networked communications system and relays the current location of the squad at all times for the entire force. The soldier can transfer the data from the GPS to his heads-up display or transpose his position on digital maps fed into his software. As a sensor, the GPS serves to refine target data for remote shooters. The system combines the accuracy of the laser-range finder and compass mounted on the Thermal Weapon Site (TWS) to give pinpoint target information.

The LW soldier's night vision capabilities are enhanced with the PVS-14. Designed for rapid transition between night vision and the naked eye, the PVS-14 sits on a flip mount attached to the ballistic helmet. Generation III technology makes the passive monocular night vision device the best available Image Intensifier (I2) night- vision device. The Thermal Weapon Site (TWS) mounted on the weapon offers the soldier infrared night-vision capability which is linked by a cable to the computer on the soldier's back. The TWS is capable of transmitting the images viewed through the weapon site to the soldier's heads-up display which allows him to observe and engage targets while he remains behind cover.

Presently, the weight of the LW rifleman's fighting load (equipment the soldier will carry when engaged in the close fight) is 82.5 pounds, and the LW leader fighting load is 85.4 pounds. The current LW rifleman designed approach load (equipment the soldier must carry to sustain himself) is 123 pounds and the LW leader approach load is 129 pounds. A soldier's fighting load accounts for the ammunition and equipment needed for the soldier to operate in accomplishment of an attack or short movement. The approach load accounts for sustainment items necessary for a longer duration mission or sustainment in the field. The LW System has passed several capabilities tests but has experienced problems passing field durability tests and air drop experiments.

LW System is not modular and does not allow soldiers to tailor their loads based upon the unit or individual missions. Every man, including the SAW and M203 (Grenade Launcher) gunners, receives a computer as a part of their load-carrying equipment regardless of the additional weight of their weapon systems and ammunition or without consideration of their likelihood to use it while on a mission. Additionally, with the LW SAW, gunners and Grenadiers would continue to use contemporary sighting and acquisition systems.[51]

Under current development by the Army as a part of the new LW System is a weapon system named the Objective Integrated Combat Weapon (OICW). According to the Infantry Center, the OICW will replace all weapons in the squad when fielded as part of the Army After Next development or Land Warrior phase II. The weapon currently in development weighs eighteen pounds with design specifications for no greater than fourteen pounds. The OICW has two weapons in one high tech package. The weapon's main round, fired from an eight-round magazine, is a 20 millimeter high-explosive hypersonic projectile, that has a 5-meter kill radius and a range of 1,000 meters. The OICW's 5.56 kinetic energy round with a thirty-round magazine constitutes the weapon's secondary system, which detaches from the main body for close combat situations.

The OICW has a computer-integrated targeting system and uses aim-point technology to acquire targets. To engage a target, the soldier places a red dot that appears in the weapon site on the target. The soldier then presses a button to laze the target, and the system computes the ballistic solution, automatically adjusts the red dot in the sight and adjusts the round's fuse to detonate 3 feet above the head of the target. The soldier then reacquires the target with the red dot from the computers adjusted point of aim and fires. The 20 millimeter HE round flies to a point three feet above the target and automatically detonates. Enemy target vulnerability and thus lethality will increase because of OICW's ability to defeat effective cover. The TSM soldier force development office predicts that this system will be ready for production and distribution in the year 2006-07. More conservative estimates call for year 2010 distribution. The weapon is also equipped with a passive (image intensifier) night scope, aiming light, and tactical flashlight for night operations.

The OICW project mangers continue to work on the production of a new generation of night vision technology called image fusion. Image fusion combines low-light television technology with image intensification and thermal night vision to produce a color night vision picture. This day and night system fluctuates rapidly from one night vision technology to the next continuously to produce a combination of all three images for the human eye.[52]

TRADOC designated Company C, 3-325 PIR at Fort Bragg, North Carolina, as the test unit for LW equipment. The current plan calls for a test of all the major components of the Land Warrior at a capstone evaluation during the Joint Contingency Force Advanced Warfighter Experiment (AWE) at JRTC in the year 2000.

Company C, 3d Battalion, 325 Parachute Infantry regiment, the LW test company, has individually tested all of the LW equipment but never simultaneously. The soldiers found the PVS-14 difficult to use. They sited difficulty adjusting to viewing the night vision out of one eye. The Close Combat Optic worked well as did the TWS in static defensive positions. MAJ Kevin Hyneman, the XO for the 2-235 PIR, relates the affects the thermal site had against his unit when they attacked the Test Company during a training exercise in the Fort Bragg MOUT site. "The night attack was preceded by heavy smoke that the 2-325 hoped to use as cover. The battalion was repeatedly repelled by well-aimed rifle fire that prevented the successful completion of the mission. Also the force within the city directed maneuver of a small counterattack units outside of the city with the TWS from defensive positions within the city to disrupt our attack. The TWS works great in the defense."[53]

Experiments conducted at the Scenario Simulations Office at the United States Infantry Center created models to evaluate the effectiveness of the Land Warrior system through simulations. One analyst said, "As evaluated against the current [weapons] systems, Land Warrior significantly increased a soldier's lethality and protection." In fact the preponderance of the evidence showed that if the Ranger force in Somalia would have been equipped with Land Warrior they would have sustained significantly less causalities.[54]

Threat and Environment

Forecasting tomorrow's geostrategic environment forms the first step in any investigation into future warfare.[55]

Army After Next Doctrine

As they have in the past, the future squad will function in the environment created by politics, social development, and environmental issues. The Army can gain insight on how the geostrategic environment will shape the National Security and Military Strategies. From this study the thesis will define what forces may oppose the United States Army and whom may have to fight in the future to support the National Military Strategy.

When examining the impact of military technology and its importance on the geostrategic environment, it is meaningful to examine the old Bible story of David and Goliath.

> It is the story that we find in the first Book of Samuel, chapter 17 during the reign of King Saul. The children of Israel are warring against the Philistines. There's a standoff between the two camps. They decide to deal with this the way one traditionally did, one champion fights the other. The Philistine champion is of course Goliath, the giant. Everybody in the Israelite camp is paralyzed with fear. In the middle of this, comes little David--a young, red-haired shepherd.
>
> David volunteers to participate in this duel. He tries on the standard military armor of the time. In fact, King Saul gives him his armor. David tries to move and he finds he cannot move. He says, "I cannot go with these, for I am not accustomed to them." And instead he falls back on a piece of advanced technology. He fishes five smooth stones out of a brook and retrieves his shepherd's sling. In the subsequent engagement between Goliath's personal armor protective system and David's precision-guided rock, the precision-guided rock wins. The ground war lasts 40 seconds, Goliath loses his head and the Israelites win the day.[56]

David's version of high-tech information age technology, a prelude to precision-guided munitions, foreshadowed the advantage that smart weapons can have over an armored clad behemoth. The Gulf War proved that precision-guided anti-tank and smart bomb systems dropped from planes can drastically change the complexion of the battlefield and allude to the RMA possible with future systems. Information age technology development costs far less than the systems required to compete with world class powers using heavy armor systems. A nation with the means can purchase this technology off the shelf to apply strap-on capabilities to current weapon systems. Additionally, as the former cash-poor Soviet Union satellites seek hard currency, many advanced military systems are for sale to the highest bidder throughout the world.[57] When discussing future threat scenario's, former U. S. Secretary of Defense Dick Cheney says, "Advanced technologies can make third class powers into first-class threats."[58]

Currently, eighteen countries have advanced precision-guided munitions, and in the first years of the next millennium that number is expected to climb into the forties. Other examples of technology proliferation are the sale of short range ballistic missiles by China and the sale of Surface to Air Missiles and Anti-Tank Guided Missiles by the former Soviet Union to other nations that the United States considers hostile.[59]

Social anarchy theorists such as Robert Kaplin contend that the artificial lines drawn by old European colonial powers in Africa and the unbridled destruction of natural resources in those areas of social and political stress will cause intense friction. He believes that war will erupt as people struggle for survival on a large scale throughout the world. Kaplin says, "Future wars will be those of communal survival, aggravated or, in many cases, caused by environmental scarcity. These wars will be sub-national, meaning that it will be hard for states and local governments to physically protect their own citizens."[60] In effect, once the nation state cannot fulfill its obligation to protect its people's liberties, groups of people will take their collective protection into their own hands. Although Americans have difficulty understanding why young men around the world so readily decide to fight we must understand the conditions in which the majority of worlds people live. Terrible living conditions around the world have created a large number of people who believe war and a barracks existence would be a step up from where they are in life.[61]

As nation states collapse, the United States will find it increasingly more difficult to determine who will be their next enemies. Nations traditionally outfit their champions to fight for their security. Traditionally, nations raise money to maintain a force to establish and maintain their security. In essence the purpose for a nation's existence is to provide secure the blessings of liberty for its people. Before national organizations existed, all suitable members (young men) of the clan, or tribe where expected to help provide for their collective defense. It is interesting to note, that in many tribal languages throughout the world, the term warrior means or is associated with "young boy." Many tribal countries without benefit of government cannot distinguish between a soldier and citizen; they are for all practical purposes one and the same. The primary purpose of national government is to protect the rights and freedom of its citizens. When nations disappear, the situation will call for a form of universal conscription to protect the members of the community or tribe, because all are vulnerable to attack without the security of standing force. This may cause the reemergence of total war albeit tribal cultures or clans will not have the means to create an arsenal of superior weapons. Total war created in this asymmetric environment may produce a product that is more dangerous than any weapon to the United States; it may inspire resolve. These tribal powers have unique and elusive centers of gravity and can strike out to affect public support, the United States' center of gravity. This sum effect will disrupt the local regional stability that the US National Security Strategy aims to support.[62]

Threats to international order will come from smaller nations that feel they have been left out of the expansive growth afforded to the worlds Western Nations.

> This new warrior class [will come] from a variety of sources: the underclass of society, -those dispossessed by a conflict, opportunists, 'true believers, patriots, zealots, fanatics, renegade military. The nonstate warrior poses a problem because he does not fight by the rules of conventional warfare: His targets are not force-oriented but are political will of his opponents; his tactics include terrorism, ambushes, kidnapping, and criminal actions; he does not keep his negotiated word.[63]

53

Few nations will pose direct conventional threats to United States sovereignty. The focus of national security will continue to be deterrence and prevention of nuclear, biological, or chemical attack and prevention or the rise to power of a hostile hegemony in Asia and Europe. Subsets of this threat include ethnic and religious conflict, epidemic health problems, environmental degradation, terrorist organizations, organized crime, and the drug trade.[64]

Many argue that the nation has effectively seen the last of the World War II and Desert Storm style maneuver wars, in their place we will witness the escalation of local and regional conflicts that will challenge our beliefs and resolve. David Woods from the Harrisburg Patriot News describes the next generation of conflict.

> in their place are mutant forms of conflict: genocide and ethnic cleansing, desperate blood-crazed savagery in arenas where the Geneva Conventions are scorned, where women and children fight, where the fallen are often mutilated, where rape and starvation are weapons as unremarkable as indiscriminate shelling and scattering of land mines in schoolyards.... These conflicts are chilling evidence of man's enthusiasm for butchery. Most of the 500,000 people slain in Rwanda in 1994 were not killed by the efficient mechanical weapons of the 20th century, but were hacked to death by machete, a slow and laborious manual job.[65]

The United States TRADOC formed a world class OPFOR to compete in free play computer simulated war game against a realistic United States armed force with year 2020 capabilities. The Army After Next War Games were open ended free-play exercises with an active and unfettered opponent (REDFOR). The REDFOR team consisted of members of the executive branch, industry, academia, military, and other government agencies. An independent contractor associated with the DOD Revolution in Military Affairs study designed the REDFOR to present an asymmetrical threat to the future US force (BLUFOR). The game showed how the poorly equipped enemy became inured to the effects of U.S. high tech weapons systems over time. "Reds learning curve rose sharply as the games progressed. Confronted by overwhelming combat power, he resorted to asymmetric responses in an effort to offset Blue's advantages. Therefore, Red moved rapidly to complex terrain--urban, suburban, and, in some cases, forests and mountains. He used his limited information warfare capabilities to slow Blue maneuver through electronic warfare and deception."[66] As time progressed, Red became stronger relative to the situation and had the ability to strike at America's resolve.

In summation, the United States as the sole global military power will face a myriad of threats to National Security, albeit most of them indirect. We will face men like Shamil Baasayev, Chechen Freedom Fighter, who personifies the threat American soldiers will oppose in the future. He is a hero with his people. He is a composite of Robin Hood and George Washington. A patriot who's sole purpose is the protection of his people's liberty and freedom. He is half terrorist, half soldier statesman, and all warrior. He was raised and trained for this purpose. He studied in Afghanistan and Pakistan, to learn the art of the guerrilla warrior from the Mujahadin. He and his people stopped the mighty Russian army in Chechnya in 1994. The Chechen people led by Shamil struck at the Russian center of gravity, their national will and resolve, by protracting the war and striking at the Russian people through the media. Shamil cares nothing for war's formal rules and is prepared to use any strategy to meet his objective. His criminal mind cares little for the laws of war.[67]

Commandant of the Marine Corps, General Krulak, predicts that, "Future war is most likely not the son of Desert Storm; rather it will be the stepchild of Somalia and

Chechnya."[68] The battle in Somalia, now referred to as the battle of Bakara Market, which occurred on 3 October 1993, is the fiercest fighting America soldiers have experienced since the Vietnam War. It was a twenty-four-hour savage battle in which eighteen American soldiers died and 60 percent were wounded. Newsman and war correspondent David Woods believes the 3 October Somalia battle, that claimed the lives of over 1000 Somalis, could be the harbinger of things to come.[69]

Doctrine

> Rapid military change is not unprecedented. But too often in the past, its driving impulse has been prior defeat. We believe effective adaptation is possible without that unpleasant incentive.
>
> Army After Next Doctrine

History shows that following a conflict, nations often prepare their forces for the war they just fought. John English author of the book On Infantry says, "[The] tactics of each war begin where those of the last war left off."[70] Correspondingly when science presents new inventions it is human nature to attempt to fit it into the existing form of warfare.[71] This dilemma has challenged military theorists throughout the history of warfare. Of particular interest are the techniques some nations have used to integrate break through technology to produce military organizations that effectively capitalize on the advantages the technology offered. While conversely some have failed to envision how the technology could advantage them using a holistic approach to change. The latter fail to achieve a marked advantage over their enemies. The former creates conditions for success.

In this approach, it is valuable to study the interwar of the 1920s and 30s. It proved the Clausewitzian theory of force development. He said political climate, priorities, and constraints drive the development of a nation's armed forces as much as if not more so than technology innovation.[72] Conversely, Virgil Ney contends that "Weaponry at all times has dictated military organization from the highest to the lowest echelons." Further he feels, "Tactics have followed weapons and their employment."[73]

Successful integration of revolutionary technology into the Armed Forces has produced a phenomena refereed to as a Revolution in Military Affairs (RMA). TRADOC refers to it, a Military Technical Revolution (MTR) and defines MTR in the following passage. "[An MTR] occurs when the application of new technologies into military systems combines with innovative operational concepts or organizational adaptation to alter fundamentally the character and conduct of military operations." TRADOC Pam 525-5 also says, "What is revolutionary about an MTR is not the speed with which the change takes place, but rather the magnitude of the change itself. Mere technological improvements do not constitute an MTR."[74]

The study of Revolution in Military Affairs is important to the essence of the Army's being. Military Forces are stuck with force structures they choose for long periods. Thus, military theorists must take exhaustive efforts to plan appropriately. The battlefield has traditionally been the best place to test the validity of doctrinal theory. Albeit training models established by the United States Army through the Combined Training Centers have decreased the reliance on actual fighting to prove our theories. It is foolish to stick to the old ways purely based on ignorance and inability or inflexibility to explore new ideas. Stagnation in thought and experiment, especially in the light of new leap ahead technology can be catastrophic.

It is similar to the experiences of the British and French during their preparation for World War II. They experimented with the use of the tank and modern technologies in the conduct of war fighting. But, as we have witnessed, they failed to incorporate their findings into organizational and operational changes and caused them to fall drastically behind the Germans at the outset of the war. Conversely, the Germans integrated the British experimentation findings into new doctrine and organizational concepts. Operational visionaries, such as General Heinz Guderian, successfully incorporated foreign misunderstood concepts into doctrine and organizational structure to create a new form of maneuver warfare. The result was a Revolution in the conduct of war that made obsolete the forces and doctrine of the last war. The cost of failure to the French and British was obvious.[75]

The Russian's coined the phrase Revolution in Military Affairs (RMA) to describe the affect produced by the introduction of nuclear weapons and ballistic missiles into warfare. Military theorists, in the Soviet Union in the late 1940's, felt that the change created by such a drastic increase of technology made all forms of past combat, as they knew it obsolete. This stymied there theorists for a short time and cause them to rapidly respond to the perceived threat of seemingly ominous systems. [76]

> The history of warfare reveals a cyclical pattern of military change in which evolving technology alternately favors attack or defense. Before the Industrial Age, such cycles alternated slowly because innovation developed and spread slowly. After the Industrial Revolution, the cycles began to accelerate, though they were still somewhat retarded by political and institutional conservatism and the uneven development of military technologies.[77]

In the years after World War II, the Soviet Union maintained a large conventional force that was capable of combined arms maneuver warfare that made the offense the dominant form of maneuver warfare in 1940. In response, the NATO allies leveraged microchip technologies to develop long range tank killing systems to counter the Soviet style blitzkrieg threat in Europe. Accordingly, the cycle of warfare once again favored the defender.

The current potential for a RMA was demonstrated by the US led coalition during the Gulf War. "The war represented the harbinger of changes that will transform warfare as profoundly as did mechanization and the introduction of nuclear weapons."[78] The potential RMA will integrate longrange precision weapons, information and space operations, as well as harnessing the power of ever-increasing composite materials and energy storage developments. These advances may create the conditions that cause the terrain of the earth to become inconsequential in relation to maneuver. Offense may again become dominant as small units move above the earth in high tech, energy efficient, cloaked vehicles that move three to five times as fast as contemporary transport.

As technology continues to improve the lethality of weapons the soldier will be forced to continue to disperse on the battlefield. This will further contribute to the empty battlefield phenomenon. The concept of deep operations has been transformed from a sequential destruction of the enemy in the deep space to shape the close fight. Theorist plan to conduct simultaneous assaults, on all his forces to stun the enemy and set him off balance, then aggressively and simultaneously pursue destruction of his center of gravity. The commander in this type of conventional to high intensity maneuver warfare desires to avoid linear face to face confrontations with the enemy. Instead, fire and maneuver

59

will take affect in a new conceptual form. Small tactical actions will occur by maneuvering to mass with the smallest possible force in a nature that is undetectable to the enemy sensors, with a massing of effects at the decisive point.[79]

Devoid of the linear boundaries that defined the AirLand Battle Doctrine of the 1980s and 90s, the term battlespace replaces the architecture of deep, close and rear operations. The physical and electronic reach of military and information systems dictates the volume of the battlespace. TRADOC, defines the ultimate objective for their implementation of the Army After Next doctrine, in terms of Strategic Preclusion. They define Strategic Preclusion as the ability to leverage the superior intelligence potential and the global reach of the United States to allow us to introduce forces anywhere in the world and rapidly strike at and destroy an enemy's center of gravity with minimal lose of life. Strategic Preclusion integrates the information technology RMA into practical terms. Army After Next theorist plan to move using such speed and such lethality that the enemy will be thrown completely off balance. The concept calls for movement of combat forces from garrisons directly into combat in a matter of days, vice the weeks and months required in the Gulf War. This will allow the United States to operate without the allowing the enemy to oppose our arrival. AAN doctrine says, "Effective preclusion will require a refined level of synchronization across the entire force, combining the effects of joint precision strike and air-sea dominance with exploitative a maneuver and contributing fire/strike from ground forces to dominate territory and the enemy."[80]

Success on the modern battlefield in the new millennium's second decade as defined by AAN will exploit the increase of velocity and speed afforded us by information age technology. The force will acquire speed (the ability to rapidly mass

60

through deployment) by the increased mobility of our heaviest ground equipment and by unburdening maneuver units of the huge logistical yoke developed in the twentieth century. Information dominance will allow American forces to bring only what they need to the fight and will free them from worse case logistics planning. The AAN's operational tempo will increase as tactical objectives are achieved in a relatively short time using a combination of light and heavy forces. The bottom line is, "The American method of war-making in the future must rely on the offensive if this nation intends, as a matter of policy, to retain the ability to strike rapidly, decide quickly, and finish wars cleanly with minimal loss of life to all sides."[81]

The model for the implementation of our future doctrine will support our current National Military Strategy of prepare, shape and respond and will remain valid through the foreseeable future. As challengers to the United States NSS attempt to interdict our foreign policy they need not match us in every area technologically. For example, opponents merely need to counter our advantages in sensor and space technology to raise the political cost of our intervention. Thus, in the future strategic environment without a single dominant threat the utility of land forces for control gains strategic control.[82]

As alluded to above, the Infantry force will regain or maintain dominance on the battlefield as part of Force XXI and the Army After Next. The only way to impose firepower on a target is to place force projectors in position to bear fires on a target. Technology gives more worth to the small independently operating Infantry force in this regard.[83] Thus, "Like his Dragoon ancestor, the Infantryman must be able to ride quickly to a suitable dismount point and there leave his conveyance, form up and press his attack from an unexpected quarter."[84]

Lastly, in the impending geostrategic environment the Infantryman must still transition to operate in the peacekeeping role. This will require him to put his weapons on stun by using non-lethal munitions. He will have to serve as the manpower required to conduct peace operations or Operations Other Than War (OOTW). Paddy Griffith, author of Forward Into Battle: Fighting Tactics Form Waterloo to The Near Future, says America has outsourced a majority of the manpower requirements to foreign nations since the Korean War to execute elements of its National Security Strategy. Attempting to develop technologically advanced weapons systems while maintaining adequate forces for higher priority contingency missions, the United States has reduced the numbers of American troops obligated to peace operations. Thus, Griffith feels the US has allowed itself to become Infantry poor.[85] AAN doctrine advocates that America will have to deploy forces to display our resolve when we participate in future coalition peacekeeping endeavors. American willingness to except a fair share of risk must be displayed by our deployment of ground forces. Army ground forces will serve as the glue that holds the coalitions together.[86]

Historic Perspective

> Most of the determinants of success in war, from courage and willpower to small-unit initiative and cool decisionmaking under fire, have little if anything to do with technology. War is at base a human affair, not a technological or scientific phenomenon; its human aspects will always predominate. High quality military personnel are therefore the bedrock of all military activity.[87]

Michael Mazarr

It is valuable to examine infantry organizational development from a historical perspective. History outlines and highlights the qualities required of the ground force to succeed. The thesis found it important to explore how nations have organized their infantry units to compete with perceived threats based on lessons from the past. History paints a clear picture of what men must endure in combat. This discipline most clearly personifies the pure essence of combat because authors can use objective facts and observations to demonstrate a point.

The asymmetrical environment defines the infantry squad's operational area. Men have dealt with its unfortunate unpleasantness throughout history some more successfully than others. Mr. S. L. A. Marshall studied the psychological and physiological effects on soldiers during war. Marshall's makes the case in <u>Men Against Fire</u> that there stands certain combat environmental occurrences that cause unique responses in man. Leaders and organization developers must consider these circumstances if a unit hopes to succeed when the bullets start flying. His studies from World War II and Korea showed that rarely more than 25 percent of all troops fired their rifles in combat unless personally supervised. Marshall receives support from James Gibson, who says, "Men by nature are gregarious, and in time of stress and anxiety they tend to 'Herd' together for mutual protection and moral support."[88] The Allies were plagued by this herding occurrence during the conduct of World War II. The problem arose from a need to disperse the troops while simultaneously keeping control of them. Marshall said that to disperse the troops effectively, they need to have close supervision or they would tend not to fight. The dilemma facing Armies then is how to maintain control of troops who increasingly have to disperse to survive. The Germans realized that his comrades sustained the soldier first and his weapon secondarily and built organizations that allowed for effective leader to led ratios.[89]

When examining how to solve the problem of supervising men in combat, John English offered his observations of the People's Liberation Army (PLA) infantry squads that fought in Korea. The PLA squads were organized into three, three-to-five-man groupings led by an inspiring communist squad leader.

> Tactically a squad so organized provided great flexibility at the lower level. It permitted a squad leader to exploit the terrain and to take advantage of the enemy situation by classic methods of fire and movement. It also provided a mechanism for assured control and constant surveillance. It is conceivable, therefore, that this basic organization, with its stress on supervision, reflected a desire to solve a long-standing problem of warfare that modern weapons have merely exacerbated, namely, the problem of getting everyone in combat units to fight.[90]

The problem of control increases as we push to disperse men further on the modern battlefield. With the increasingly nonlinear, dispersed, decentralized operations that are forecast by Force XXI and Army After Next operations, it could create a sense of loneliness and fear that is unparalleled in previous operations. Soldier isolation could put distinct limits on how we organize the force. Joint Vision 2010 expects to remedy the problem with training but understands that there are limits to man's abilities. It says, "Our leaders' and warriors' training, initiative, resilience, and understanding will be essential to success in future operations. Their physiological and psychological limitations also will make them a vulnerable part of our warfighting system."[91]

History has shown that close combat is a physically challenging endeavor. Many theorists have realized that the soldier as a member of the squad fights the battles and wins the war. Therefore it deserves appropriate attention. Nations need to prepare their squads for combat by setting the conditions for success. Thus, a disproportionate amount of energy should go into development of weapons to fit the squad not vice versa. General George Patton said, "Wars may be fought with weapons but they are won by men. It is

64

the spirit of men who follow and the man who leads that gains the victory." To stress a point about the importance of the infantryman, Virgil Ney quoted COL Sprung, Brigade Commander during World War II.

> It is important to remember that only the soldier function is primary. It is the soldier who presses the trigger, throws the grenade, pulls the lanyard on a gun. The soldier is the great doer of the army's work. The entire vast machine behind him exists only to see that he pulls the trigger or throws the grenade at the right time and place ... It is characteristic of an army that its plainest members are its most important members.[92]

Armed forces must organize, arm and properly train, and prepare their infantry because it is the base on which the Army is built.

Many armies accredited with developing outstanding infantry units avoid becoming inured with technology. The German Army in World War II, despite the new technology and doctrine of maneuver warfare, placed great emphasis on the physical and mental toughness of their soldiers. They created squad competitions, called Wehrsport, that stress basic combat skills of machine gunners, marksmanship, and physical fitness in an attempt to foster small unit development. As a measure of their toughness, German infantry units were able to move up to thirty miles a day for several days on end and remain combat effective.[93]

Two other examples of nations that trained using physical toughness to cope with the stresses of combat to bring about success on the battlefield include the Japanese Army in World War II and the Israeli Defense Force (IDF) in 1956. The Japanese infantry was trained to be self-reliant and to live off of small rations. They stressed physical training and conducted foot marches of up to twenty-five miles a day.[94] Likewise, prior to 1956 the IDF stressed marksmanship, physical training and leader training to prepare for combat. A standard test for IDF NCO candidates was to complete a 40-mile march in eight and one-half hours.

Liddell Hart dedicated considerable effort to the study of the infantryman as a member of a small organization. He advocated adoption of the framed rucksack as the individual load carrier and suggested that load-bearing equipment should not hang below the hips to avoid impeding the running and movement of the soldier.[95] His insight is further illustrated by this passage about the infantry he wrote during the inter-war years.

> The revived infantryman would be "tria juncta in uno--stalker, athlete, and marksman." Equipped with a lighter rifle, to alleviate ammunition supply, and trained to a high standard in fieldcraft, he would be capable of destroying enemy machine gun and antitank positions through stealth and deadly accurate small-arms fire.... Unlike his Great War counterpart, however, he would not be a beast of burden carrying 70 pounds of personal kit; rather, he would carry but one-third of his own weight. Dressed as an athlete and "light of foot," he would also be "quick of thought" and capable of acting on his own or as part of an independent team.[96]

The Red Army, during the same period, was an outstanding example of organizational proficiency. They traveled perhaps as light or lighter than any army of modern times. So important was the battlefield mobility of the infantryman that they went into combat with the bear essentials. An indicator of the extremes they took, Russian soldiers were not issued scabbards for their bayonets. By their adherence to infantry principles, they stymied a technologically superior German force in the close terrain of the Pripet marches and in the cities throughout the Eastern Front.[97]

Combat in Vietnam proved again that men fighting unencumbered by excessive weight could defeat a superior force with greater tactical mobility.[98] The Viet Cong guerillas and North Vietnamese Army carried far less equipment than their American counter parts. Thus they were able to strike and disappear into the dark often without decisive engagement with the American superior firepower.

In John English's discussion of contemporary issues, he states that the infantry can once again compete with the tank by capitalizing on the integration of precision guided munitions into the mobile, adaptable Infantry. Even though many of the great skills of the basic infantryman have been lost in mechanized units, the light infantry and airborne units will keep have kept them in relenace. American military theorists agree and TRADOC Force XXI supports English's thesis, "Technology offers much, but American soldiers of the future, as in the past, will be called upon to be flexible and versatile. They will be counted upon to display mental agility and American ingenuity as they seek alternative methods--often low technology--to cope with the circumstances that surround them."[99]

---

[1]Virgil Ney, <u>Organization and Equipment of the Infantry Rifle Squad: From valley Forge to R.O.A.D.</u> (Fort Belvoir, VA: United States Army Combat Developments Command, 1965), 74.

[2]Ibid., 10-11.

[3]Ibid., 74.

[4]Ibid., vii.

[5]Ibid., 30-32.

[6]Ibid., 3.

[7]Ibid., 74.

[8]Infantry Conference, <u>Report of Committee "B" on Tactics and Techniques,</u> (Fort Benning, GA.:The U.S. Army Infantry School, 1946), T-18 cited hereafter as the <u>Report of Committee "B"</u>.

[9]Ney. 54.

[10]Report of Committee "B", 5-6.

[11]Ibid., T-18.

[12]Ibid., T-18.

[13]John A Whittenberg, A Study of the Infantry Squad TOE (Fort Monroe, VA: U.S. Army Continental Command, 1956), 74.

[14]Ibid. 75.

[15]United States Army Combat Developments Command, Optimum Composition of the Rifle Squad and Platoon. (Fort Ord, CA: Combat Developments Command, 1961), 16.

[16]Ibid. 20, 79-80.

[17]U.S. Army Infantry School, Rifle Squad and Platoon Evaluation Program (Fort Benning, GA: Office of the Chief Evaluator, 1961), 25.

[18]Ibid., 37.

[19]Ibid., 37.

[20]Ibid. 38.

[21]Ney, 66.

[22]T. A. Williams and Horace E. Homesley Jr., Small Unit Combat experience Vietnam, 1966-1967 (Fort Benning, GA: U.S. Army Combat developments Command, 1967), 1.

[23]Ibid., 15-25.

[24]U.S. Army Combat Developments Command, Infantry Rifle Unit Study, IRUS (Fort Benning, GA: Combat Developments Command, 1969). 17.

[25]Ibid., 17.

[26]U.S. Army Combat Developments Command, Executive Summary Phase II, Infantry Rifle Unit Study 1970-1975 (Fort Benning, GA: Combat Development Command, February 1970), 5-6.

[27]Ibid., 7.

[28]John L. Romjue, The Army of Excellence: The Development of the 1980s Army. (Fort Monroe, VA: United States Army Training and Doctrine Command, 1993), 15-21.

[29]LTC John Medve, USA, Knowledge and Speed: The Annual Report on The Army After Next Project to the Chief of Staff of the Army (Fort Monroe, VA: United States Army Training and Doctrine Command, 1 August 1997), A-6.

[30]Alvin Toffler, The Third Wave. (New York: Bantam Books, 1989). General theme of the book.

[31]Christopher Bellamy. The Evolution of Modern Land Warfare: Theory and practice. (London: Routledge, 1990), 38.

[32]Ibid., 37.

[33]Ibid., 37.

[34]John A English,. On Infantry. (New York; Praeger, 1981). p. 3.

[35]Ibid., p2.

[36]Medve, A-2.

[37]Frederick R. Strain, "The New Joint Warfare," Joint Force Quarterly. (Autumn 1993), 24.

[38]Medve, A-2.

[39]Paddy Griffith, Forward into Battle taken form Galen B. Jackman. Col. Holistic Review of Infantry, United States Army Infantry Center. (Fort Benning, GA: Combined Arms and Tactics Directorate, February 94), MOI 6.

[40]John A. English. On Infantry. New York: Praeger, 1981,147.

[41]S. J. Lewis. Forgotten Legions: German Army Infantry Policy 1918-1941. (New York: Praeger, 1985), 66.

[42]Medve, A-1.

[43]Ibid., 177.

[44]Ibid., 185.

[45]Department of the Army, Army Training and Doctrine Command, TRADOC Pamphlet 525-5. <u>Force XXI Operations: A Concept for the Evolution of Full-Dimensional Operations for the Strategic Army of the Early Twenty First Century</u> (Fort Monroe, VA: U.S. Army Training and Doctrine Command, 1 August 1994), 3-9.

[46]Chris J.Yaniger. "Next-Century Land Warrior Equips to Fight Unseen Forces." <u>Signal Magazine</u>, (March 1996). [Online] Available at http://www.us.net/../ March96/Next-mar.html., accessed 31 August 98, 1.

[47]GEN William W. Hartzog, USA, <u>Land Combat in the 21st Century</u> (Fort Monroe, VA: U.S. Army Training and Doctrine Command, 1994), [Online] available http://www.monroe.army.mil/cmdpubs/landcmbt.htm 6 October 1998, 1.

[48]English, 201.

[49]Mazarr, Michael, J. <u>The Military Technical Revolution, A Structural Framework</u> (Washington D.C: Center for Strategic and International Studies, March 1993), 42.

[50]Medve, 25.

[51]MAJ Jeff Bovais, USA, TSM Soldier, The Infantry Center, Fort Benning, GA. Telephonic Interview by author, 19 February 1999, Fort Leavenworth, Kansas, authors Notes.

[52]MAJ Erik Fletcher, USA, Small Arms Combat Development Manager, The Infantry Center, Fort Benning, GA. Telephonic Interview by author, 18 February 1999. Fort Leavenworth, Kansas, authors Notes.

[53]MAJ Kevin A. Hyneman, USA. Regimental Operations Officer, 2d BDE 82d Airborne Division, Fort Bragg, North Carolina, telephonic Interview by author, 21 February 1999. Fort Leavenworth, Kansas, authors Notes.

[54]MAJ Tony Carbone, USA, Scenario Simulations Office, The Infantry Center, Fort Benning, GA. Interview by author, 19 Feb 1999. For Leavenworth, Kansas. Telephonic Interview authors Notes.

[55]United States Army Training and Doctrine Command, <u>Annual Report on the Army After Next</u> (Fort Monroe, VA: U.S. Army Training and Doctrine Command, 7 December 1998), 1, online available at http://www.tradoc.army.mil/dcsdoc/aan.htm., accessed 20 January 1999, cited hereafter as <u>Army After Next</u>.

[56]Prof Eliot Cohen, "Military Technology and Man," in <u>Proceedings from the Conference on Manpower & Technology at the End of the 20th Century</u>. 23 February

1998, ed. Jim Colbert (Washington, DC: Jewish Institute for National Security Affairs, July 1998), 3.

[57]Colonel (Ret.) Graham H. Turbivillle, William W. Mendel and Dr. Jacob W. Kipp, "The Changing Security Environment." Military Review 57, (May-June 1997), 6.

[58]Commander, Joint Warfighting Center, Concept For Future Joint Operations: Expanding Joint Vision 2010 (Fort Monroe, VA: Joint Warfighting Center, May 1997), 14.

[59]Gordon Sullivan and James Dubik, Envisioning Future Warfare (Fort Leavenworth, KS: United States Army Command and General Staff College, 1995), 3.

[60]Robert D. Kaplin, "The Coming Anarchy," The Atlantic Monthly (February 1994), 74.

[61]Ibid., 79.

[62]MAJ Raymond C. Finch, III., USA. "A Face of Future Battle: Chechen Fighter Shamil Basayev" Military Review. (May-June 1997), p 39.

[63]TRADOC Pamphlet 525-5. Force XXI Operations: A Concept for the Evolution of Full-Dimensional Operations for the Strategic Army of the early Twenty First Century Fort Monroe, VA: Department of the Army, Army Training and Doctrine Command, 1 August 1994), 2-4, cited hereafter as Force XXI Operations.

[64]Turbivillle, 8.

[65]Woods, David, "The Rangers: Can American Kids Kill With the Best?" Harrisburg Patriot News, 1 November 1998, n.p.

[66]Medve, 14.

[67]Finch, 35.

[68]Ibid., 33.

[69]Woods, n.p.

[70]English, 52.

[71]Christopher Gabel, "Introduction to Lesson 12A." The History of Warfighting: Theory and Practice (Fort Leavenworth, KS: The United States Army Command and General Staff College, 1998 –1999), 138.

[90]Ibid., 171-172.

[91]Commander, Joint Warfighting Center, Concept For Future Joint Operations: Expanding Joint Vision 2010, (Fort Monroe, VA: Joint Warfighting Center, May 1997), 17.

[92]COL G. M. C. Sprung, The Soldier in Our Time, Philadelphia: Dorrance and Company, 1960, 68.

[93]English, 59.

[94]Ibid., 156.

[95]Ibid., 39.

[96]Ibid., 38-39.

[97]Ibid., 45.

[98]Larry H. Addington, The Patterns of War Since the Eighteenth Century. Bloomington, IN: Indiana University Press. 1994, 300.

[99]Force XXI Operations, 3-23.

CHAPTER 5

CONCLUSIONS AND RECOMMENDATIONS

> Having burned out the enemy's circuits, blinded him with
> lasers, deafened him in the ether, you still have to have forces
> capable of occupying this territory and forcing him to "do your
> will" ... When both sides have disabled their C3I, brains, and
> nervous systems, they will revert to tanks, then to rifles, and
> finally to rocks.

> Christopher Bellamy

When examining the possibilities for the Infantry squad organization, it becomes readily apparent, based on the scope of this investigation, that we must bound the options for consideration. To accomplish this, the study will limit the variables for the squad organization to the size, measured in numbers of people, and its internal organization based on fire teams. While defining the scope of options for the organization it is then important to first identify the equipment and weapons the soldier of the squad will carry prior to comparison. Establishing the clothing and equipment of the individual soldier is vital because it traditionally impacts heavily on the capabilities of the unit and thus how the identified organizations will compare against the selection criteria. This study will not compare the variety of options for squad equipment and weapons mix, but instead advocate the optimal set based on the analysis in chapter 4.

Next the study will limit the comparison of squad organizations to three based on the historical investigation in chapter 4 and contemporary restrictions. By limiting the comparison it allows the study to keep the problem manageable and relevant. The limitations that I will impose on squad size and rank structure also make this study and its recommendation feasible to contemporary organizational modeling based on the future Army force structure and continued Army downsizing.

The rank structure of the squad will remain relatively unchanged. The squad leader will remain a staff sergeant and sergeants will continue to lead fire teams. Based on Force XXI and Army After Next doctrine many could certainly argue that the average Staff Sergeant is not experienced enough to execute the extremely decentralized operations on the digital battlefield. Although we will not investigate the squad leader's training requirements for the force of 2015, it suffices to say that as the Army force evolves so too the resilient, adaptable Staff Sergeant will adapt to the new environment. The Army may have to adjust the promotion criteria to the staff sergeant rank based on the cognitive abilities and maturity that the position will require. It will also be confirmed that the most important quality the squad leader will need is the ability to be an effective direct level leader. Our base line contemporary staff sergeants clearly demonstrate this requirement.

Historic examination reveals that a leader's span of control should not exceed 5 soldiers or units in combat. The Sergeant fire team leader should not be an exception to this rule, thus I will limit the size of any fire teams considered to five men. The first recognized leadership position in an Infantry organization is the Sergeant Team Leader. He is the only true fighting leader in the Army and is the epitome of the ultimate direct leader. But because of his maturity he is relatively unskilled in the decision-making process and he will continue to lead by example more than by direction. His motto of "follow me and do as I do" will remain relevant well into the next century, but the effectiveness of his supervision will increase based on his ability to talk to each of his

75

soldiers via the internal squad radio net. Based on the relative inexperience of the Sergeant and the ability to direct individual actions over the radio his potential to lead larger numbers of personnel will remain unchanged.

Next I will impose a twelve-man size limitation to the squad. By definition the size of the organization is limited to the number of men the squad leader can directly supervise. Based on my experience, a squad leader can ably handle a squad of 10 men. This is based on personal observations while serving as a company commander. Weapons squad leaders, who are often the most experienced squad leaders in the company, could ably supervise the 9 men assigned to their units but were tested when that number was raised to 12. This observation is based on the 10 man weapons squad being increased to 13 with the addition of a three man anti-tank team.

Equipment

Projecting the squad's equipment and weapons is critical to further define the possibilities of organizational structure. Although the squad's equipment should match the organizational development and not dictate the structure, it is important to establish the equipment available because it impacts heavily on the squad's capabilities. Traditionally the squad has had to adapt to the equipment manufactured for it. Ergonomics has rarely affected the development of Infantry systems, but hopefully that will change with the development of the soldier systems under the Land Warrior design. The Squad's equipment and weapons will directly affect the capabilities of the squad. Information age technology will improve the squad's communications ability, which includes his ability to sense for larger weapons systems, and will improve the individual soldier's firepower potential. Information age technology also has the potential to constrain the squad and adversely effect other qualities such as situational awareness, logistics and mobility.

The best protection for the infantryman in battle is his ability to move quickly and stealthily, utilizing cover as he moves. All equipment to include his basic load can not exceed one third of his body weight. There can be no exception to this rule. The members of the squad must be able to carry all organic individual and squad equipment, weapons and ammunition using this weight limitation. Developers of equipment systems must therefore, employ a holistic approach to the integration of all equipment the Infantryman carries so that it can fit onto the soldier by design. Again, the assault load, defined as the load the soldier will carry when in contact with the enemy, cannot exceed 60 pounds or 1/3 the average mans body weight.

Nothing is affected more by the weight of equipment the soldier carries than his mobility. During the Normandy landing in World War II the soldiers on the initial assault were criminally overloaded, John English observed this.

> The American soldier carried more than 80 pounds [during the first waves in the amphibious assault], and any careful examination of photographs of British and Canadian troops waddling ashore on that day will reveal that they, too, were weighted down. The D-day assault definitely showed that a direct relationship exists between an infantry soldier's tactical performance and the load he carries on his back…. He should have been as lightly equipped and fleet as an athlete…. It is indeed sadly ironic that many of these soldiers carried on their backs several cartons of cigarettes (the killing kindness of a concerned welfare officer no doubt) and sufficient rations for three days. Subsequent surveys showed that in the excitement of action most men did not even eat during the first day of fighting.[1]

To make matters worse it is usually the staff planner or organizational level leaders that prescribes unrealistic solder's loads to facilitate contingency planning

77

without appreciation for what impact it has on the soldier's mobility. In his book <u>The Solder's Load</u>, S. L. A. Marshall says,

> no amount of training will ever condition an infantryman to carry excessive weight. Nor is it a sensible staff solution to suggest that the innate common sense of the soldier will invariably cause him to discard unnecessary items after the shooting starts. On the beaches of Normandy, this was impossible, and the combat line consequently floundered under the weight of bangalore torpedoes that were never exploded, gas equipment that was never used, and ladders that would have been useful had there been a cliff.[2]

Tactical mobility equates to protection for the Infantryman. The faster and more efficiently a soldier can move from cover to cover while crossing the killing zone the better are his chances for survival. There is a direct relationship between causality rates and soldier exposure time to enemy fire. Exposure time (time it takes to move from one covered position to the next) is proportionate to the soldier's load. As Virgil Ney aptly wrote, "The rifle squad must have only elements of maximum battlefield mobility. All its members must be capable of short dashes at high speed in order to cross zones exposed to hostile fire."[3]

Weight of equipment also impacts on the ability of the squad to sustain itself. Supporting our statement above, Liddell Hart advocates a soldiers load weight ceiling of no more than one third of his body weight. Anyone who has ever moved a great distance under fire simulated or real, will tell you that even one-third of a soldier's weight treads on limiting his mobility beyond expectable levels. The average man weighs between 160 and 170 pounds,[4] therefore the soldier's fighting load cannot exceed 60 pounds. Logistics materiel and equipment for the squad cannot add to this weight without nullifying the principles of Hart and Marshall. In the analysis of doctrine in chapter 4 it is evident that the future Army squad will operate increasingly further away from direct support.

To continue, the equipment the squad will possess will be defined. Each member of the squad will carry an internal squad radio with advanced convenience features. The hands-off speaker headset will integrate into the helmet to limit the number of moving parts the soldier must manipulate to operate the communications system. The internal communication within the squad will greatly increase their situational awareness and assist in overcoming the problems of supervision in combat that S. L. A. Marshall describes in Men Against Fire.

During my command in Company A, 3d Ranger Battalion, several squads in the company thought that the internal squad radio was so vital to achieve high proficiency in combat that they purchased radios with their own funds. The radio-equipped squads consistently performed better than the remainder of the squads in the company because the commands from the squad leader to the unit were executed quicker and with less energy expended from the squad leader. The Battalion Commander, Lieutenant Colonel Michael Ferriter was so impressed by the performance of the internal communication equipped squads that he decided to purchase a platoon's set of individual radios for the battalion to test under different training scenarios. Each member of the test platoon was issued a radio. Squad leaders were able to give commands during maneuver exercises effortlessly. Every member of the squad reacted favorably and morale improved, because they were constantly apprised of the situation. They displayed improved proficiency during live and blank fire exercises. Traditionally, because of the noise associated with live fire training a squad leader expends a great deal of energy communicating with his team leaders. The squad radios allowed squad leaders to issue instructions to their team leaders without moving from cover. The radio also allowed the squad leaders to quickly adjust their plans if the situation required. The end result was that squad leaders spent considerably more time solving the tactical problem rather than trying to communicate and the squad's performance increased two or three fold. The addition of internal communication within the squad will become a great combat multiplier for the infantry squad and will favorably effect its capabilities.

To integrate the Infantry squad electronically into the Army force, the squad will have to carry some form of a computer to process data and to send friendly information to higher headquarters. To integrate the squad into the Army Force's relevant common picture it will need to carry at least two computers with Heads Up Displays (HUD). This system should be carried by soldiers who will act as RTOs. This "information warrior" will transmit the information gathered by members of the squad using digital communications. Similar to any RTO he will have to monitor the current situation and transmit information continuously, albeit using a HUD, but as a result similar to those experienced by his RTO ancestor, he will have substantially less situational awareness. He will also have less maneuverability because of his load. It is important to note that a sophisticated computer, similar to most privately owned personal computers, will not be used to its full potential and any duplication of resources is a waste of the squad's precious load carrying ability. The squad computer will process data from higher, to include the transition of maps, graphic, orders and intelligence. It also will allow the squad to communicate digital information to higher headquarters in the form of visual images taken with an attached digital pencil camera, as well as administrative information. The computer will also facilitate relaying images captured by one solider in the squad via his pencil camera, to all the other the members of the squad.

Other factor, point to limiting the issuance of computers to all members of the squad. The first is the large energy supply needed to operate the system. The Land Warrior Computer presently requires two lithium batteries for each twelve hours of service. The batteries weigh over a pound a piece that would significantly increase the soldier's load. Lastly is the marginal benefit that the soldier would gain from having a computer while he is moving toward or operating on the objective. To remain alert foot soldiers must pay distinct attention to the surroundings. The HUD for the most part would not be used or may become a distracter. The Infantryman must use all of his senses to survive in the harsh environment that close combat presents and cannot focus on the information on a heads up display, operate a computer and effectively function as a member of a fire team.[5]

The Infantryman's uniform will unfortunately not change much from what he wears today although it will provide the comfort and quality that pro athletes enjoy. The Infantryman will eventually maneuver into battle in a powered suit that provides him additional strength to carry advanced weapon systems and that will accelerate him rapidly at 10 times the rate of the Infantryman using only human power. But, progress in the development of powered suits and thermally controlled garments have not made advances that would make the large-scale distribution possible for the Infantry force in the early part of the twenty first century.

We will create a uniform and protective equipment for the Infantryman that is comparable in fit and comfort to a professional football or hockey player's. His battle

81

fatigues will be made of more durable light weight fabrics that dries quickly and has the durability to hold up to the fatigue of combat. This uniform will have spaces to insert lightweight polymer knee and elbow pads, similar to those found in a football player's uniform. The Infantryman's boots will be made of rugged lightweight fabrics with a flexible soft sole that stands up to punctures and gives the soldier superior traction and comfort for rapid acceleration.

The soldier's web gear will be comprised of a vest made of lightweight material that allows the soldier to tailor his load to the mission and that distributes the weight of his equipment over his hips not his shoulders. Nothing will hang below the hips that will prevent the soldier from running. No piece of equipment will dangle off of the soldier at any time. Everything carried will attach to the web gear and will be modular, using quick snap attachments. The protective mask will decrease in size and have power blowers to facilitate rather than encumber combat operations in close contaminated terrain. The protective mask carrier will fit conveniently on the Load Bearing Vest (LBV) without creating a menace for the soldier.

To give the soldier adequate protection in the close fight we will provide him with a protective vest that integrates with the LBV. The detachable front plate will be capable of stopping a 9 mm round at close range.[6] The helmet will continue to be made of Kevlar but the chinstrap and internal webbing will resemble a football or motorcycle helmet. The helmet must also serve as a mount for the HUD, Night vision devices, a digital camera and radio headset. Eye protection will resemble the Bole styled sunglasses, but will provide laser protection, a sturdy frame and an elastic headband for security.

The water carrying system will resemble the modern modular Camel Back. The Camel Back system allows the soldier to carry a two-quart soft pouch on his back with an 18 inch hose that allows for hands off water intake. The soft water pouch will detach and snap on the back of the solder. The soldiers water hose will adapt for use with the protective mask. This system will eliminate the need for canteens and move them off of the soldier's hips and provide him a better more accessible water source and increase his maneuverability.

The squad will be equipped with the helmet mounted Image Fusion night vision goggles. These night vision devices will afford the soldier the advantages of Image intensification, low light television and Infrared technology. Thus he will be able to identify thermal images during day or night while moving. He will also be able to see through most forms of concealment.

The M-249 light machine gun (SAW) helped to relieve the squad of the relative weight of the older machine guns such as the BAR and improved mobility. But as we know, the SAW still constrains the mobility of the entire squad in the close fight. Also, as the squad attempted to capitalize on the night vision technology proliferation in the Army during the eighties, it struggled with how best to fight and maneuver the SAW at night. In addition to the weight of the system itself, the automatic rifleman, was burdened by a heavy night vision image intensifier scope, the PVS-4, which mounts on the top of the weapon's feed tray cover and inhibits its operation. This system prohibited effective rapid assault by the fire team because the SAW gunner could only see when looking through his scope in the prone. Recently, in an effort to improve the SAW gunner's abilities and situational awareness in the close fight, units have mounted the

PAQ-4C aiming light to the weapon system and outfitted the SAW gunner with passive night vision device mounted on his helmet. The PVS-7Ds or PVS-14s improve the SAW gunner's situational awareness and allows him to maneuver at the same rate as the rest of the squad when in contact.

As the force evolves we must continue to improve the mobility of our primary fire suppression asset in the squad. To do this the entire squad will carry the fourteen pound Objective Integrated Combat Weapon (OICW). The OICW will allow the automatic rifleman to maintain his mobility and provide suppression for the squad with a fraction of the rounds required by the SAW. As described in chapter 4 the OICW will increase the firepower potential of each rifleman, but to achieve the qualities of suppression the OICW will have to undergo modification. The weapon will have to integrate aiming light technology into the system to afford engagements in close contact using the head mounted night fusion goggles. Developers will also have to equip the OICW with a direct fire mode to effectively engage targets as a suppression weapon. The direct fire mode will enable soldiers to engage targets that have overhead cover provided by a bunker, building window or door. This will make the Automatic Rifleman as a specially trained member of the squad obsolete in traditional terms. Although he will have to carry an additional load of 20 millimeter projectiles and fire his weapon primarily on the direct fire mode to continue to provide the primary source of suppression for the squad, he will not require the additional training that the SAW gunner require. Using the OICW a soldier will achieve suppression by fire effects caused by accurate 20 millimeter HE fire and not hundreds of rounds of 5.56 millimeter fired from a light machine gun. Although the individual 20 millimeter rounds are heavier than the old 5.55 millimeter round there will be an overall weight savings to the squad.

To improve the survivability and medical care for the soldier, each man will carry a personal body monitor that will transmit his vital statistics to his squad leader on demand. He will also carry a 911 bandage to facilitate better on site medical treatment and life sustainment.

As indicated by the threat and future doctrine analysis in chapter 4 the trends in geostrategic environment will call for an increased US involvement in OOTW scenarios and operations involving Strategic Preclusion. This situation will demand dominance of the terrain by Infantry units in a traditional role as fighter and as a sensor for larger weapon systems. The majority of fighting will occur in the vicinity of cities or rugged terrain, thus the infantry squad must be able to operate effectively the typical light infantry environment. Even serving as a sensor the infantry squad may have to fight to establish itself in a favorable position to acquire a target designated for destruction.

Operations will continue to become more decentralized and require more flexibility from leaders at low levels and make decisions based on intent and relevant common picture vice direct control by verbal orders. There may be limits on how decentralized we can operate based on logistics and the abilities of small unit leaders to internalize the cognitive qualities required to effectively operate in the conditions outlined in AAN Doctrine. Thus in the foreseeable future the squad will remain part of the Platoon and be limited to operating with in the span of control of the platoon leader.

The study of the Infantry Squad evolution allowed us to examine the critical qualities the squad had to possess in contemporary or historic terms. These qualities modified based evolving threat and doctrine are still relevant to the evaluation of a future

squad organization because the general principles of Infantry tactics will remain constant

through the next 15 years. Even when used as a sensor for larger more lethal weapon

systems, the squad will have to maneuver and fight to gain position advantage on the

enemy. We will examine the qualities as discussed in Chapter 4 and test them against the

impacts of evolving threat, doctrine and other basic guiding combat principles. The

selection criteria for squad composition in order of importance are; lethality (Firepower),

resiliency, maneuverability or control in combat (fire and maneuver), leader to led ratio,

dispersion, and logistics.

It is important to address these criteria in priority as this order of importance has

an impact on the effectiveness of the organization. Although all the criteria in our

comparison have an impact on the squad organization some have more relative worth

than others. The most important quality is that of lethality or firepower, which has been

confirmed in all applicable studies up to now. Firepower is the measure of suppression

potential based on numbers and types of weapon systems carried by the squad. The

ability to achieve fire superiority facilitates maneuver and rapid destruction of the enemy.

The importance of organic firepower to establish dominance in the close fight is clear.

All studies since the development of the BAR have forcefully advocated that the core of

the squad and or fire team be the light machine gun. In Vietnam War Infantry studies,

many combat veterans called for the integration of the M-60 machine gun into each squad

and or the fire team in order to ensure fire superiority for the squad. In a traditional sense

the automatic weapon is the key to establishing the suppression necessary to conduct fire

and maneuver in the close fight. With the proven need for automatic weapons in the squad, leaders have faced challenges on how to conduct rapid maneuver with an automatic weapon that is heavy and cumbersome. Basically lethality has been often gained at the cost of mobility in the squad. Based on the authors personal experience involving hundreds of live and blank fire simulations with Infantry squads, it is clear that the squad can only move as fast as its slowest member, which inevitably is the man carrying the machine gun. The introduction of the OICW maintaining lethality will have less effect on mobility. So the squad's firepower will increase directly with the number of systems integrated into the unit.

Resiliency is the ability of the squad to sustain anticipated combat losses without losing its identity or capability to operate as designed.[7] The Vietnam experience showed that squads lost their ability to effectively conduct fire and maneuver when it was attrited below seven men.[8] In effect the study showed that the fire team lost its ability to provide adequate firepower for suppression and lost its identity when it dropped to three men or less. Army After Next doctrine and the uncertainty of the asymmetrical combat environment may determine that the criteria of resiliency as the foremost quality for squad selection. Decentralized operations coupled with the dispersion required to survive in a potentially lethal battlefield will pull the squad away from their base of direct fire support. The resiliency calls for robust squads that can receive several causalities and continue their mission while caring for their wounded. Most studies express that the typical squad in combat can expect to operate at 25 percent of its original strength because of manning difficulties and combat attrition. The number of personnel in the Fire Teams directly influences the quality of resiliency.

Maneuverability or control in combat is the measure of a squad leader's ability to effectively maneuver his unit and respond to changing conditions presented in combat. It is effected by the number of units or individuals the squad leader is required to maneuver and his ability to communicate with them. The smaller the number, the better his ability to control the maneuver of his unit under fire. With the adaptation of the inter-squad radio this quality will remain important but will be less of a factor than firepower or resiliency.

Mobility is measure by the squad's ability to move to an objective dismounted and the physical ability to conduct movement under fire. It has been one of the critical evaluation criteria in past squad organizational studies. It is vitally important that the members of the squad maintain the ability to sprint from cover to cover to rapidly close with the enemy and to enhance their protection. Mobility is vitally important when considering what equipment the squad should carry or in comparing squads that employ different weapons types. As discussed previously, with maximum lethality as the ultimate goal of past squad organization, the allocation of heavy weapons to increase lethality adversely affected mobility. Since we have determined that we will provide all members of the squad with the same weapons and equipment this quality will remain the same for each organization and will not receive further consideration in this study.

Leader to led ratio is defined by the number of leaders allocated for every soldier in a unit. The lower the leader to led ratio the closer the supervision the soldiers of a unit will receive. S. L. A. Marshall advocated a low leader to led ratio to overcome the natural herding instinct in all soldiers. This ratio is an increasingly important factor considering the trend toward decentralized operations of future combat. It also contributes to success in Operations Other Than War, where each soldier's actions have potential strategic implications.

Dispersion is the ability of the unit to protect itself from massed enemy fires by physical separation. Dispersion is directly effected by the ability of small units to physically separate and is constrained by the need for control. Traditionally, an increase in dispersion among the members of the unit has had an adverse affect on the ability to mass fire and control units in contact. S. L. A. Marshall says that the human herding qualities limit dispersion potential, because of the directly supervise soldiers to force then to fight effectively. The more leaders in charge of smaller teams within an organization increase the unit's dispersion potential.

Logistics is defined as the ability of the squad to support itself without assistance from its higher headquarters. This equates to the amount of equipment or supplies required for use by the squad to conduct its mission as designed. Logistics is affected by the amount of equipment or supplies the squad calls for to complete its mission divided by the number of personnel in the unit to carry them. It also is a factor of the squad's ability to treat, sustain and transport its wounded to an evacuation area. Again more members in the squad is generally better using this criterion.

Comparison

The Infantry Squad's capabilities are affected by many factors such as the physical strength in people, weapons types, equipment, training, organization and rank of the members of the squad. Each of these variables that in total equate to the composition of the squad, affect the squad capabilities and impact on its ability to meet desired

89

criteria. Major General Armistead Meade wrote about the importance in considering size of the Infantry squad in his article Those Who See the Whites of Their Eyes and is quoted by Virgil Ney, "To make a squad large or small should not be the objective in considering its organization. Instead, the size of the squad should be the result of organizing it to meet certain essential criteria." Meade further explained that it is imperative that the squad have resiliency to assist, not hinder, its higher headquarters in the accomplishment of its missions.[9]

In 1994, The Infantry School at Fort Benning Georgia under Major General White, conducted a study to review the Infantry organization for implementation in the twenty-first century Army. Colonel Galen Jackman authored the study titled The Holistic Review of Infantry with guidance from the Commanding General of the Infantry Center. MG White aptly acknowledged that technology should not independently drive organizational structure. He said, "I am looking for the synergy of yet unfielded equipment and untested doctrine to help me determine the right structure, weapons, and tactics for our Infantry."[10] Major General White's vision based on the examination of threat and evolving doctrine and consideration of technology should be used as a starting point for future force development. Major General White called this a holistic approach to the problem of force development. He also defined the future role of the Infantry in the United States Army as "the principal ground combat force, a finder for precision systems and as manpower resource for Operations Other Than War (OOTW)." Major General White's vision agrees with the evolving threat and doctrine as defined in chapter 4, and I will use it as the mission statement for the Infantry squad organization in the year 2015. It is important to understand that the Major General White's, definition of the

90

infantry's mission is markedly different than the traditional narrowly focused mission. The traditional mission is, "To close with the enemy by means of fire and maneuver in order to destroy or capture him, or to repel his assault by fire, close combat and counter attack." This delineation of an Infantry force away from strictly a fighting force is key to this and other future studies considering force structure.

Chapter 4 outlined the future threat to national security and the doctrine that the Army will employ to successfully operate against those threats. As TRADOC Pam 525-5 states, the most likely employment of the future infantry force will continue to be into OOTW scenarios. But it is also clear that the Infantry, as the rest of the Armed Forces, should prepare for the combat in high intensity conflict and create an organization that is flexible enough to respond to any crisis. Additionally TRADOC Pamphlet 525-5 states that the best deterrent to conflict is a force capable of fighting and winning on the high intensity battle.[11]

The study limited the options for consideration to three distinct squads. It is certain that the squad must consist of subunits, Fire Teams, if it is to maintain the ability to fire and maneuver. Thus, we should only consider squads consisting of fire teams. Then determine the number fire teams and the number of men in each fire team to create the optimal organization based on criteria. The three squad organizations that are considered are; the nine-man "Army of Excellence" squad consisting of two fire teams of four men each, a ten-man squad with three fire teams of three men each, and a 11 man squad with two fire teams of five men each.

The nine-man squad has advantages in maneuverability and control in combat for it has the least number of units and smaller teams than the eleven man squad. It has logistics as a disadvantage, simply because it has the least strength in people.

The ten-man, three fire team squad has advantages over the other organizations by having a superior leader to led ratio and the best potential with small teams to disperse. It rates poorly in lethality, resiliency, and maneuverability. Even though it has ten men, it is organized in three subunits, which presents a larger control challenge to the squad leader. It will be difficult to get all teams into the fight and suppression by a team will only allow for the fire power potential of three weapons. This squad lacks resiliency. One loss to a fire team will destroy its ability to operate as designed.

The eleven-man squad with two five-man fire teams has advantages in firepower, resiliency and logistics. More men have positive effects on those criteria without breaking the span of control restriction. And indeed within reason more is better. The squad has a relatively poor leader to led ratio and lacks the ability to disperse, but technology, particularly the squad internal radio will help to mitigate those challenges.

To illustrate the results of the comparison, a decision matrix is presented below. Lower numbers are favorable. A pairwise comparison was used to weight the factors in the comparison and are listed from left to right in their order of importance to the squad as described above. This comparison achieved a consistency ratio of 99.41 percent.

TABLE 1. SQUAD RELATIVE VALUE COMPARISON MATRIX

Weight	5.24	3.06	3.06	1.69	1.69	1.0	
	Lethality / Firepower	Resiliency	Maneuver / Control	Leader to Led Ratio	Dispersion	Logistics	Total
9 Men 2 Teams	2	2	1	2	2	3	29.403
10 Men 3 Teams	3	3	3	1	1	2	39.453
11 Men 2 Teams	1	1	2	3	3	1	25.541

Notes: Relative Value Matrix: Less is better.   Consistency Ratio of 99.41%

The eleven-man organization scored superior and is the composition of the organization recommended for the infantry in the year 2015. Tactics for this squad would remain relatively unchanged even with the addition of the new equipment that the squad will carry. Several battle drills would change but for the most part infantry tactics will remain the same. The largest change between this squad and the nine-man AOE Squad would be the addition of the fifth man who would serve as a fighting "Information Warrior" for each of the fire teams and the loss of the Automatic Rifleman and the Grenadier.

Recommendations

The development of Land Warrior System must adhere to a weight limitation that most theorists agree upon. Generally the system with all of its components can not weigh more than sixty pounds. The system must be modular so that a unit can tailor its load to account for changes in the tactical situation. Additionally all components of the soldier's equipment as described above must be developed in concert with a central approving authority so that it is compatible for wear on the ergonomically designed LBV. This includes the protective armor. On some operations such as long range infiltration the benefit of protection would be outweighed by the ability to move light. Furthermore the commander should be allowed to make the decision on where he will except risk to the force.

Until the development of the OICW the Land Warrior computer and integrated M4 with TWS should not be issued to every soldier in the Infantry squad in its present configuration, particularly because of its weight of the system itself and the required batteries. A modular system would allow for leaders to decide who will carry the computer. The cable that connects the weapon to the HUD is cumbersome and will inhibit the soldier's mobility. The design specifications should require the TWS or compatible system to communicate via air waves, similar to a way chord less key boards relay data to modern computer systems.

The issuance of computers to every member of the squad is redundant and unduly overburdens the squad with weight in both equipment and batteries. The members of the squad are adequately receive and send information through the Information Warrior that will feature a portable display for shared viewing. As described above it is projected that most of the members of the squad will only use the computer during troop leading procedures, so we should not burden the squad with the essentially excess load during the fight. As described above, one member of each team should serve as the "Information Warrior" for the team. The information warrior will adopt a role similar to the traditional

RTO. Only with the internal squad communications the Information Warrior would not have to stay within arms reach of the leaders. He could rely information over the radio and the entire team could hear would receive the update. This soldier also would carry the high tech information gear and could act as a sensor for larger weapons as the in essence serve as the teams Forward Observer. This will allow most of the members of the team to operate without the burden of the weight of the system and drastically reduce the battery consumption rate of the squad. Lastly this reduction in distribution would allow for wider initial distribution of the Land Warrior Computer throughout the Army.

The Army's infatuation with technology has the potential to deprive the force of the critical Infantry required to win a fight in close terrain. A side effect of the costly development of high technology weapon systems is a proportionate decrease in manpower to save resources. As Jeffery Record writes in the article, *The October War: Burying the Blitzkrieg*, "Unfortunately, the price of Western technological superiority has been a growing disinvestment in numbers. In fact, the real cost of procuring ever fancier, more expensive--and, therefore, fewer--aircraft, ships an armored fighting vehicles may be force, albeit elegantly equipped, that are simply too small to survive probable rates of attrition."[12] This reflects the establishments desire to maintain standing Division and Brigade guideons while depriving commanders of the trained Infantry forces required to operate effectively. In Race To the Swift, Simpkin supports Mr. Record theory. He suggests that there is a point of diminishing returns on the cost paid in soldiers used to pay for force development. Clearly we restrict the number of troops and multipliers in a unit based on costs to the organization as a whole. Thus we tend to shrink the size of a unit to just barely adequately its assigned mission. We must not mortgage today's readiness for future potential. As a consequence this directly translates into the size and shape of tactical units in the organization of an army. The United States is in danger of substituting technology for personnel strength, which is an extremely dangerous proposition with the impending threat of the twenty-first century.[13]

The Armed Forces may have become inured to the value of an infantry attack as a result of success of the RMA styled Gulf War. We must not forget what Simpkin says, "Nobody, I think, has any doubt about the effect of a successful infantry attack. The objective is cleared of enemy, and enemy who do not get away become casualties or prisoners. The defending fore is 'destroyed' in the common usage of the word." This notion is reflective of the Israelis attitude in the 1973 Arab Israeli War voiced by John English, "The harsh truth was that mesmerization with firepower and armor had induced, if not a myopic view of the worth of infantry in general, at least a benign neglect of valued infantry skills."[14] In fact Hendrick, the hero of Robert Heinlein's Starship Troopers, reflected the feeling of some contemporary theorist mesmerized by technology in the following passage from the book. "If we can use an H-bomb ... isn't sort of ridiculous to go crawling around in the weeds, throwing knives and maybe getting yourself killed ... and even losing the war ... when you've got a real weapon you can use to win? What's the point in a whole lot of men risking their lives with obsolete weapons when one professor type can do so much by pushing a button?"[15] But, historically it is always the rugged, adaptable infantry that secures a nation's victory.

---

[1]John English, On Infantry, New York; Praeger, 1981, 139-140.

[2]Ibid., 140-141.

[3]Ibid., 40.

[4]Mennes, Kellie, R.D., Dietitian Health Care. Interview by author, 10 March 1999, Fort Leavenworth, Kansas. Authors notes.

[5]MAJ Alex Montieth, USA, Deputy Chief Experimental Force Coordination Center for the Army Warfighter Experiment in April 1997, Telephonic Interview by author, 5 October 1998. Fort Leavenworth, Kansas. Authors notes. Alex stated that the only time the computer was used during the fights at the AWE was during Troop leading procedures and after the fight. It did not in any way assist the squads during the fight.

[6]Infantry School has developed a light weight vest with ceramic plate that stops 9 mm rounds.

[7]English, 40.

[8]United States Army Combat Developments Command. Infantry Rifle Unit Study, IRUS. Fort Benning, GA: Combat Developments Command, 1969, n.p.

[9]MG Armistead D. Meade, USA. "Those Who See the Whites of Their Eyes," United States Army Infantry School Quarterly. 46, No. 3, July 1956: n.p.

[10]COL Galen B.Jackman, Holistic Review of Infantry. (Fort Benning, GA: Combined Arms and Tactics Directorate, United States Army Infantry Center, February 1994), n.p.

[11]TRADOC Pamphlet 525-5, Force XXI Operations: A Concept for the Evolution of Full-Dimensional Operations for the Strategic Army of the early Twenty First Century, Fort Monroe, VA: United States Army Training and Doctrine Command, 1 August 1994, 2-10.

[12]Jeffery Record, "The October War: Burying the Blitzkrieg." Military Review 56, April 1976, 19-21.

[13]Richard Simpkin, Race to the Swift: Thoughts on 21st Century Warfare, London: Brassey Defense, 1985, 134-136.

[14]English, 189.

[15]Robert A. Heinlein, Starship Troopers, New York; Ace Books, 1987, 51.

BIBLIOGRAPHY

United States Army Studies and Reports

Commander, Joint Warfighting Center. Concept For Future Joint Operations: Expanding Joint Vision 2010. Fort Monroe, VA: United States Army Training and Doctrine Command, May 1997.

Department of the Army, Training and Doctrine Command, TRADOC Pamphlet 525-5. Force XXI Operations: A Concept for the Evolution of Full-Dimensional Operations for the Strategic Army of the early Twenty First Century. Fort Monroe, VA: United States Army Training and Doctrine Command, 1 August 1994.

Dupree, Robert and Horace Homesley Jr., A History of United States Infantry Squad and Platoons, 1935 – 1967. Fort Benning GA: United States Combat Development Command, 1967.

Gibson, James M., Organization of the Rifle Squad. Fort Benning, GA: Tactics Department, The US Army Infantry School, 1954.

Havron, Dean M.. A Research Study of Infantry Rifle Squad TOE. Fort Monroe, VA: Headquarters, Continental Army Command, 1956.

Hartzog, William W., GEN, USA. Land Combat in the 21st Century, Fort Monroe, VA: United States Army Training and Doctrine Command, 1994.

Infantry Conference. Report of Committee "B" on Tactics and Techniques. Fort Benning, GA: The U.S. Army Infantry School, 1946.

Jackman, Galen, B. Col. Holistic Review of Infantry. Fort Benning, GA: Combined Arms and Tactics Directorate, United States Army Infantry Center, February 94.

Kirin, Stephen, J. COL USA, Study Plan For The Division XXI Advanced Warfighting Experiment." Fort Monroe, VA: United States Army TRADOC, October 96.

Leonhard, Robert R. FORCE XXI How to Fight. Power Point Presentation. Fort Monroe, VA: Joint Venture Office, DCSCD, TRADOC, 1996.

Medve, John, LTC, USA. Knowledge and Speed: The Annual Report on The Army After Next Project to the Chief of Staff of the Army. Fort Monroe, VA: United States Army Training and Doctrine Command, 1 August 1997.

Mazarr, Michael, J. The Military Technical Revolution, A Structural Framework. Washington D.C: Center for Strategic and International Studies, March 1993.

Ney, Virgil. Organization and Equipment of the Infantry Rifle Squad: From valley Forge to R.O.A.D. Fort Belvoir, VA: United States Army Combat Developments Command, 1965.

Record, Jeffery. Ready For What and Modernized Against Whom?: A Strategic Perspective on Readiness and Modernization. Carlisle Barracks, PA: U.S. Army War College, 1994.

Romjue, John L. The Army of Excellence: The Development of the 1980s Army. Fort Monroe, VA: United States Army Training and Doctrine Command, 1993.

Sullivan, Gordon, and James Dubik. Envisioning Future Warfare. Fort Leavenworth, KS: United States Army Command and General Staff College, 1995.

United States Army. Weapons Systems, Washington D.C: U.S. Government Printing Office, 1998.

_____. Battlefield Automation: Army Land Warrior Program Acquisition Strategy May Be Too Ambitious. Fort Benning GA: Abstracts of GAO Reports and Testimony, NSID-96-190, 11 September 1996.

United States Army Combat Developments Command. Infantry Rifle Unit Study, IRUS. Fort Benning, GA: Combat Developments Command, 1969.

_____. Executive Summary Phase II, Infantry Rifle Unit Study 1970-1975. Fort Benning, GA: Combat Developments Command, February 1970.

United States Army Combat Developments Command. Optimum Composition of the Rifle Squad and Platoon. Fort Ord, CA: Combat Developments Command, 1961.

United States Army Infantry Center. Combat Developments. Fort Benning, GA: United States Army Infantry Center, 1998.

United States Army Infantry School. Holistic Review of the Infantry. Fort Benning, GA: Combined Arms Training and Doctrine Department, 1994.

_____. Infantry 2000. Fort Benning, GA: Combined Arms Training and Doctrine Department, 3 October 1991.

_____. Rifle Squad and Platoon Evaluation Program. Fort Benning, GA: Office of the Chief Evaluator, 1961.

_____. Summary of Projects. Fort Benning, GA: Small Arms Division, Directorate of Combat Developments, October 1998.

United States Military Academy. Science and Technology for Leaders of the 21st Century. West Point NY: The United States Military Academy, 1998.

Whittenberg, John A. A Study of the Infantry Squad TOE. Fort Monroe, VA: U.S. Army Continental Command, 1956.

Williams, T. A. and Horace E. Homesley Jr., Small Unit Combat Experience Vietnam, 1966-1967. Fort Benning, GA: U.S. Army Combat developments Command, 1967.

Published Articles

Abrams, John N., GEN. "Training the 21st-Century Soldier." Army Magazine, February 1999. 25.

Anderson, Jon R. "Fighting with new purpose: Marines 'new' experimental unit looks at future wars." Navy Times. 44, no. 31 (8 May 1995): 30.

Bond, Brian and Alexander, Martin. "Liddell Hart and De Gaulle: The doctrines of Limited Liability and Mobile Defense." Edited by Paret, Peter Makers of Modern Strategy from Machiavelli to the Nuclear Age., Princeton, New Jersey: Princeton University Press, 1986. p. 623.

Cohen, Eliot, Prof. "Military Technology and Man." Proceedings from the Conference on Manpower & Technology at the End of the 20th Century. 23 February 1998, ed. Jim Colbert (Washington, DC: Jewish Institute for National Security Affairs, July 1998), 3-8.

Cook, Nick. "Scenario 2015: How Science Shapes War." Jane's Defense Weekly 27, no. 23 (11 June 1997): 47.

Dunlap, Charles J., Jr., Col. "21st-century land warfare: Four dangerous myths." Parameters 27, no. 3 (Autumn 1997): 27–37.

Finch III, Raymond, C., MAJ, USA. "A Face of Future Battle: Chechen Fighter Shamil Basayev." Military Review 77, no. 3 (May-June 1997): 33-41.

Fitzsimonds, James, R. and Jan M. Van Tol,. "Revolution in Military Affairs." Joint Force Quarterly 4, (Spring 1994): 24–31.

Gabel, Christopher. "Introduction to Lesson 12A." The History of Warfighting: Theory and Practice. Fort Leavenworth, KS: The United States Army Command and General Staff College, 1998–1999. 137-138.

Green, Brian M., and John M Gallagher, "Reviewing the Army's Mine, Countermine, Nonlethal Weapons, and Demining Programs." Research Development, Acquisition, Army RD&A. Washington, D.C: (January-February 1999): 46-47.

Kaplin, Robert D. "The Coming Anarchy." The Atlantic Monthly. 273, No.2. (February 94): 44-76.

Killebrew, Robert B., Col. "Army After Next: TRADOC's (Training and Doctrine Command) crystal ball eyes the service's shape beyond Force XXI." Armed Forces Journal International 134, no.3 (October 1998): 22–24.

Mahnken, Thomas G. and Barry D. Watts. "What the Gulf War can (and cannot) Tell Us About The Future of Warfare." International Security 22, no. 2 (fall 1997): 151-162.

Marshall, Andrew. "Opening Remarks." Proceedings from the Conference on Manpower & Technology at the End of the 20th Century. 23 February 1998, ed. Jim Colbert (Washington, DC: Jewish Institute for National Security Affairs, July 1998), 1-2.

Meade, Armistead, D. Major General USA. "Those Who See the Whites of Their Eyes." United States Army Infantry School Quarterly. 46, No. 3, July 1956: np.

Meadows, Sandra I. "Logistics load makes land force too slow for 21st century warfare." National Defense 82, no. 530 (September 1997): 18–19.

Metz, Steven. "Which Army After Next? The strategic implications of alternative futures." Parameters 27, no. 3 (autumn 1997): 15–26.

Peters, Ralph, MAJ. "Culture of future conflict." Parameters 25, no. 4 (inter 1995–1996): 18–27.

Peters, Ralph, MAJ. "War in 2020." Parameters 21j no. 4 (winter 1991–1992): 115–118.

Record, Jeffery. "The October War: Burying the Blitzkrieg." Military Review 57, April 1996, p 19-21.

Sherman, David. "Causalities and the Rifle Squad." Marine Corps Gazette 75, no. 10 (October 1991): 71–72.

Shirley, Terrence, Eugene. "21st Century Mobile weapon Platform." Research
Development, Acquisition, Army RD&A. (January-February 1999): 27-28.

Strain, Frederick, R. "The New Joint Warfare." Joint Force Quarterly. (Autumn 1993):
17-24.

Thie, Harry, Dr.. "United States Military Human Capital at the End of the 20th Century."
Proceedings from the Conference on Manpower & Technology at the End of the
20th Century. 23 February 1998, ed. Jim Colbert (Washington, DC: Jewish
Institute for National Security Affairs, July 1998): 29-35.

Turbivillle, Graham, H. Colonel (Ret.),.William W. Mendel and Dr. jacob W. Kipp,
"The Changing Security Environment." Military Review 57, (May-June 1997):
5-10.

Wood, David. "The Rangers: Can American Kids Kill With the Best?", Harrisburg
Patriot News. (1 November 1998): np.

Wood, David. "Leadership Lost: The cost of shutting down the jungle training center."
Army Times. (1 March 1999): 12-14.

Yaniger, Chris, J. "Next-Century Land Warrior Equips to Fight Unseen Forces." Signal
Magazine. (March 1996); available fromhttp://www.us.net/../March96/Next-
mar.html; Internet accessed 31 August 1998.

Books

Addington, Larry, H. The Patterns of War Since the Eighteenth Century. Bloomington,
IN: Indiana University Press. 1994.

Bellamy, Christopher. The Evolution of Modern Land Warfare: Theory and practice.
London: Routledge, 1990.

Brodie, Bernard, and Fawn M. Brodie. From Crossbow to H-bomb: The evolution of the
weapons and tactics of warfare. Bloomington, IN: Indiana University Press,
1973.

English, John A. On Infantry. New York; Praeger, 1981.

Griffiths, Paddy. Forward into Battle: Fighting tactics from Waterloo to Vietnam.
Sussex: Anthony Bird, 1981.

Gudmusson, Bruce I. Stormtropper Tactics: Innovation in the German Army 1914-1918.
New York: Prager, 1989.

Hart, Liddell. <u>Thoughts on War</u>. London: Faber and Faber, Ltd., 1944.

Heinlein, Robert A. <u>Starship Troopers</u>. New York: Ace Books, 1987.

Keegan, John. <u>The Face of Battle: A Study of Agincourt, Waterloo and the Somme</u>. Middlesex: Penguin Books, 1976.

Lewis, S. J. <u>Forgotten Legions: German Army Infantry Policy</u>. New York: Praeger, 1985.

Marshall, S.L.A. <u>Men Against Fire</u>. Gloucester: Peter Smith, 1978.

Pounelle, Jerry. <u>Go Tell the Spartans</u>. New York: Basin Books, 1981.

Simpkin, Richard. <u>Race to the Swift: Thoughts on 21st Century Warfare</u>. London: Brassey Defense, 1985

Toffler, Alvin. <u>The Third Wave</u>. New York: Bantam Books, 1989.

Monographs

Funk, David E. MAJ, USA. "Tactical Dislocation: Force XXI Doctrine or Just Another Pretty Theory?" Monograph, School of Advanced Military Studies, 1997.

Hughes, Stephen E. MAJ, USA. "The Evolution of the U.S. Army Infantry Squad: Where Do We Go From Here? Determining the Optimum Infantry Squad Organization for the Future." Monograph, School of Advanced Military Studies, 1995.

James, William T., Jr. MAJ, USA. "From Siege to surgical: The evolution of urban combat from World War II to the present and its effect on current doctrine." MMAS Thesis, Command and General Staff College, 1998.

Jones, Brian D., MAJ, USA. "Force XXI: What are the Risks of Building a High Tech, Narrowly Focused Army?" SAMS Monograph, Command and General Staff College, 1996.

Melody, Paul E., MAJ, USA. "The Infantry Rifle Squad: Size is Not the Only Problem." Monograph, School of Advanced Military Studies, 1990.

Morehouse, David, A., MAJ, USA. "A New Strategic Era: A Case for Non-Lethal Weapons." MMAS Thesis, Command and General Staff College, 1992.

Newell, Peter A., MAJ, USA. "US Army marksmanship training for Infantry rifle engagements during MOUT a study of instinctive behavioral requirements." MMAS Thesis, Command and General Staff College, 1997.

O'Neil, Mark J., MAJ, USA. "Advantages and Disadvantages of night fighting command and control instruments at the tactical level." MMAS Thesis, Command and General Staff College, 1998.

Rainey, James, E., MAJ, USA. "Sharpening the Tip of the Spear: Is the Light Infantry Squad the Right Size for the Future Battlefield." Monograph, School of Advanced Military Studies, 1998.

Ramos, Enrique, MAJ, USA. "Analysis and Significance of the Battle of Kursk in July 1943." MMAS Thesis, Command and General Staff College, 1995.

Penkston, Bobby Ray, MAJ, USA. "The Logistics Implications of the Prussian Use of Railroads For Strategic and Operational Mobility." MMAS Thesis, Command and General Staff College, 1995.

Interviews

Bovais, Jeff, MAJ, USA, TSM Soldier, The Infantry Center, Fort Benning, GA. Telephonic Interview by author, 19 February 1999. Fort Leavenworth, Kansas. Authors notes.

Carbone, Tony, MAJ, USA, Scenario Simulations Office , The Infantry Center, Fort Benning, GA. Telephonic Interview by author, 19 February 1999. Fort Leavenworth, Kansas. Authors notes.

Fletcher, Erik, MAJ USA, Small Arms Combat Development Manager, The Infantry Center, Fort Benning, GA. Telephonic Interview by author, 18 February 1999. Fort Leavenworth, Kansas. Authors notes.

Hyneman, Kevin, A. MAJ USA. Regimental Operations Officer, 2d BDE 82d Airborne Division, Fort Bragg North Carolina. Telephonic Interview by author, 21 February 1999. Fort Leavenworth, Kansas. Authors notes.

Mennes, Kellie, R.D., Dietitian Health Care. Interview by author, 10 March 1999, Fort Leavenworth, Kansas. Authors notes.

Montieth, Alex, MAJ USA, Deputy Chief Experimental Force Coordination Center for the Army Warfighter Experiment in April 1997. Telephonic Interview by author, 5 October 1998. Fort Leavenworth, Kansas. Authors notes.

Internet Sites

Battlefield Automation: Army Land Warrior Program Acquisition Strategy May Be Too Ambitious. Abstracts of GAO Reports and Testimony, FY 96. NSID-96-190, 11 September 1996; available from http://www.gao.gov/AindexFY96/abstracts /ns96190.htm; accessed 31 August 1998.

Dismounted Battle Space Battle Lab. available from http://wwwbenning.army.mil/ fbhome/DBBL /dbbl.htm; accessed 5 October 1998.

Hasenauer, Heike, "The 21st Century Soldier.", Soldiers Magazine. (August 1995); available from http://www.georgetown.edu/grad/CCT/505/projects/21cen.html; accessed 6 October 1998.

"One Digital Day." Fortune Magazine.; available from http://www.pathfinder.com/ fortune/onedigitalday/alt/updates/updateo6.htm; accessed 31 August 1998.

Small Arms Division.; available at http://www.bennig.army.mil/dcd/sad.htm; accessed 20 October 1998.

Hartzog, William W., GEN USA, Land Combat in the 21st Century. Fort Monroe, VA: U.S. Army Training and Doctrine Command, nd; available at http://www.monroe. army.mil/cmdpubs/landcmbt.htm; accessed 6 October 1998.

United States Army Infantry School. Summary of Projects. Fort Benning, GA: Small Arms Division. Directorate of Combat Developments, nd; available at http://www.benning.army.mil/dcd/sad.htm; accessed 20 October 1998.

Annual Report on the Army After Next. Fort Monroe, VA: United States Army Training and Doctrine Command, 7 December 1998. available at http://www.tradoc. army.mil/dcsdoc/aan.htm; accessed 20 January 1999.

Briefing

GEN DePuy, William, E. "The Past, the Present and the Future Airland Battlefield." Speech for the Infantry Officers Advanced Course Students. Fort Benning, GA. October 1989.

www.ingramcontent.com/pod-product-compliance
Lightning Source LLC
Chambersburg PA
CBHW081400280526
45788CB00009B/2942